wood sculpture

chaim gross

THE TECHNIQUE OF

wood sculpture

WITH PHOTOGRAPHS BY ELIOT ELISOFON
AND OTHERS

ARCO PUBLISHING COMPANY, Inc.   New York

This edition published 1965 by
ARCO PUBLISHING COMPANY, Inc.
219 Park Avenue South, New York, N.Y. 10003

Library of Congress Catalog Card Number: 64-17382
ARCO Catalog Number: 1199
Book designed by Sidney Solomon
Manufactured in the United States of America

Second Printing, 1966

contents

acknowledgments

FOR information and facts on woods and equipment, aside from their use in sculpture, grateful acknowledgment is made to:

TIMBERS OF TROPICAL AMERICA, by Samuel J. Record and Clayton D. Mell, Yale University Press, New Haven, Conn., 1924

TIMBERS OF THE NEW WORLD, by Samuel J. Record and Robert W. Hess, Yale University Press, New Haven, Conn., 1943

A MANUAL OF TIMBERS OF THE WORLD, by Alexander L. Howard, Macmillan and Company, Ltd., London, 1920

FROM FOREST TO FURNITURE, by Malcolm H. Sherwood, W. W. Norton Co., New York City, 1936, for both statistical data and interesting and colorful background material on woods

THE MATERIALS OF SCULPTURE, by Jack C. Rich, Oxford University Press, New York City, 1947

WOOD HANDBOOK, U. S. Department of Agriculture, U. S. Government Printing Office, 1940

CATALOG, HANDBOOK OF HARD WOODS, LOGS, LUMBER AND VENEERS, of the J. H. Monteath Co., Inc., New York City, and especially to MR. GEORGE H. DAYTON, Vice-President, for his personal interest and willing assistance

MR. CHARLES F. BINGLER, for his personal help and the catalog of tools issued by his company, Charles F. Bingler & Sons, Inc., New York City

PAMPHLET of Behr-Manning, Division of Norton Co., Troy, N. Y. entitled "How to Sharpen Tools"

Fig. 1. The sculptor measures a block from a lignum vitae log at the lumber yard where the log has been seasoning for several years. The dealer is preparing to gouge off a bit of the discolored surface to reveal the wood's true color and surface grain.

Fig. 2. Further examination of the lignum vitae block's density and of its grain as revealed by the cross cut at the end.

Fig. 3. The first step before the carving begins. The sculptor making study drawings from a model of one of several poses.

Fig. 4. The sculptor sketching another pose. Movements and forms for the final composition are selected from the sketches of several poses.

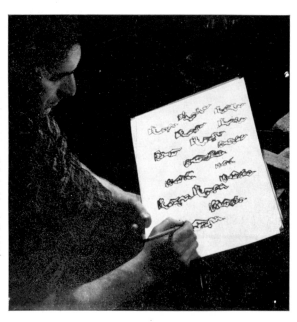

Fig. 5. Making rough sketches that begin to suggest the final composition, after studying sketches from the nude.

Fig. 6. The finished figure "Acrobats Balancing" on the work bench and, arranged next to it, the tools used to carve it. Variations and duplicates of some of the tools are shown in the racks in the upper left. Each type of tool and equipment can be easily identified in the illustration on the next page.

BASIC WOOD SCULPTURE TOOLS
AND EQUIPMENT

1. One inch (deep) gouge, for preliminary chipping
2. One inch gouge, (less curved) for finer chipping
3. One inch gouge, for hardwood
4. ⅝ inch gouge, for softwood
5. ½ inch gouge, for fine detail carving
6. Small (deep curved) gouge, for detail carving
7. Small (deep curved) fish tail gouge for detail carving
8. Six inch riffler for small varied shapes
9. Seven inch riffler for small varied shapes
10. Eight inch riffler for small varied shapes
11. Twelve inch riffler for fine finishing and curves
12. Six inch rasp for finishing details
13. Eight inch semi-curved rasp for partly rough surfaces
14. Ten inch rough rasp for eliminating rough tool marks
15. Ten inch rasp for finishing details
16. Eight ounce medium-light lignum-vitae mallet
17. Twelve ounce heavy lignum-vitae mallet
18. Steel scraper for smoothing curved areas
19. Steel scraper for smoothing large areas
20. Steel scraper for smoothing surface of wood
21. Sandpaper
22. Steel wool
23. Arkansas oilstone for maintaining a keen edge on tools while working with them
24. Oilstone for drastic sharpening of tools
25. Oil for use on oilstones
    Bench and vise (not shown in picture)
    A low stand with a stationary or revolving platform top (not shown in picture)

This basic set of tools and equipment will serve virtually all the needs of advanced workers as well as beginning wood sculptors. New tools are usually replacements of these or the occasional addition of a size or shape not used before.

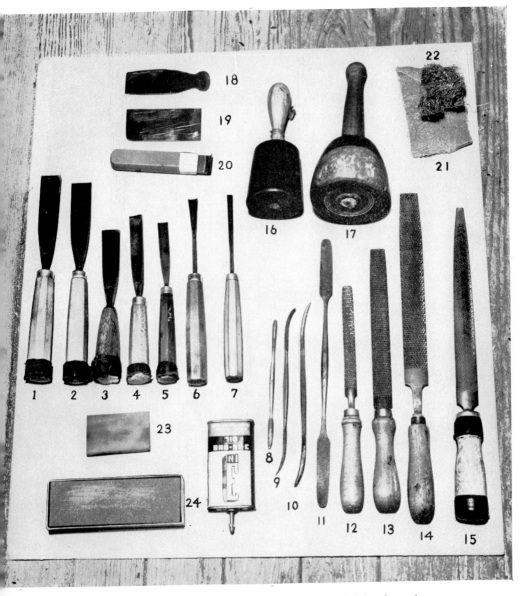

Fig. 7. Basic Wood Sculpture Tools and equipment recommended by the author.

APPLYING THE SKETCH
TO THE BLOCK

Fig. 8. The block of lignum vitae wood.

Fig. 9. Using white chalk, the sculptor roughly draws the general shape of the composition on the block of wood.

Fig. 10. The first deep cuts to remove the surplus wood are shown being made with a 1-inch deeply curved gouge which is being driven into the wood by means of a 16-ounce lignum vitae mallet. *At this stage, protection for the eyes is absolutely essential* as each large, jagged chip flies off in an unpredictable direction.

Fig. 11. The results of cutting in three areas close to the limiting chalk lines with the 1-inch gouge.

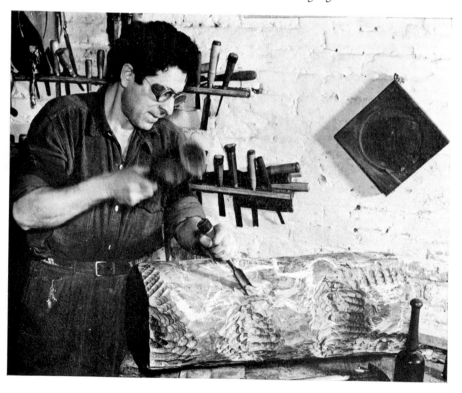

Fig. 12. Cutting away the ridges between the deep gouge marks — which results in a less rough surface — and at the same time cutting a little deeper into the block.

USING A FLATTER GOUGE

Fig. 13. The rough, drastic cutting with a wide, deep gouge having been accomplished, the sculptor selects a flatter gouge to go all over the surface of the carving to cut a little deeper and continue to produce a somewhat smoother surface.

Fig. 14. With a great deal of the wood cut away, the sculptor can now stand the block on its base and start the work of bringing out the final form with one of the flatter gouges.

HOW THE MALLET AND GOUGE
ARE HELD

Fig. 15. The correct way to grasp the gouge and the mallet. Note the angle at which the large gouges are directed at the wood to cut across the grain.

Fig. 16. Halfway roughed-out log of wood with deep gouge marks still covering the surface. Here the sculptor begins the more detailed search for the forms and rhythm he intends to achieve.

Fig. 17. At this stage the figure subject has begun to be recognizable. The changes in the method of carving are evidenced by the fact that the figure is now carved at the sculptor's eye level. He uses a ¾-inch gouge, and an 8-ounce mallet.

Fig. 18. When the gouge marks become short and shallow, smoothing is begun by using the flat and rounded 10-inch wood rasp.

Fig. 19. Here, and in the illustration above, is shown the way both hands must be used to control the rasp. Two steps in the process of smoothing can be seen, the unsmoothed shallow gouge marks, and the smoother rasped areas, which also show the very narrow, fine ridges left by the rasp.

Fig. 20. The next to the last smoothing process is done with a sharp edged object such as a flat piece of steel or an edge of broken glass.

Fig. 21. After a last smoothing with steel wool, the color and grain of the wood are at last revealed at their best by the application of "French Finish" with a soft cloth

THE
FINISHED FIGURE

Fig. 22. A side view of "Acrobats Balancing" showing the play of light and shade on the many plane surfaces, enhanced by interesting adaptation of varying grain formations and colors.

A SAMPLING OF FINISHED PIECES
BY THE AUTHOR, SHOWING A VARIETY OF
WOODS AND TECHNIQUES

Fig. 23. "Mother and Child at Play," by Chaim Gross (1937). 6 feet high. Palo blanco (whitewood). In the collection of the Newark Museum, Newark, N. J.

Fig. 24. "Renee," by Chaim Gross (1941). Applewood. 14 inches high.

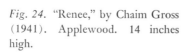

Fig. 25. "Acrobatic Dance," by Chaim Gross (1933).
Mahogany. In the collection of Mimi Gross.

Fig. 26. "In Memoriam — My Sister Sarah, Victim of Nazi Atrocities," by Chaim Gross (1947). Cocobolo wood. 6 feet high.

Fig. 27. "Head to Toe," by Chaim Gross (1941). Light yellow Cuban mahogany. In the Collection of the Norton Gallery, Palm Beach, Florida. 34 inches by 28 inches.

Fig. 28. "Self Portrait," by Chaim Gross (1933). Walnut. 22 inches high.

Fig. 29. "Juliette," by Chaim Gross (1942). American walnut. In the collection of Abbott Laboratories, Chicago, Illinois. 18 inches high.

Fig. 30. "Bird's Nest," by Chaim Gross (1941). Lignum vitae wood. 42 inches high.

Fig. 31. "Lillian Leitzel," by Chaim Gross (1938). 52 inches high. Macassar ebony. In the collection of the Metropolitan Museum of Art, New York City.

Fig. 32. "Twins," by Chaim Gross (1943). 6 feet high. Sabicu wood. In the collection of The Whitney Museum of American Art, New York City.

Fig. 34. "Girl With a Mirror," by Chaim Gross (1928). 20 inches high. Snakewood. In the collection of Mimi Gross.

Fig. 33. "Girl On a Wheel," by Chaim Gross (1940). 27 inches high. Lignum vitae wood. In the collection of the Metropolitan Museum of Art, New York City.

Fig. 35. "Offering Bearer," funerary model, from Thebes, XI Dynasty, from the tomb of Mehenkwetre, of wood, painted. A girl bearing a basket of meat and live duck. In the collection of the Metropolitan Museum of Art.

Fig. 36. Perfumery Spoon. Girl Swimming and Holding Duck. Egyptian, possibly 5000 B.C. A masterful example of Egyptian woodcarving. Grace and charm refute the concept that Egyptian art — and life — dwelt only on sombre themes of death, majesty, and eternity. The lyrical, playful quality of this woodcarving is achieved by simple forms, boldly conceived, rejecting petty miniature fussing. This is true of all fine woodcarving in all periods. (Cairo Museum).

Fig. 37. "Virgin and Child," Austrian 13th Century, School of Vienna. The Virgin theme expressed with human intimacy in a masterpiece of medieval woodcarving. Photograph, courtesy of the E. & A. Silberman Galleries, Inc.

Fig. 38. "Angel," English c. 1475, from the tomb of Alice, Duchess of Suffolk, Oxfordshire, in the Ewelme church. Photograph, courtesy of the Metropolitan Museum of Art, New York City.

Fig. 39. "Virgin and Child with Donor," German 14th Century, a detail of a choir stall from Wessenberg in the Schnutgen Museum, Cologne. A fine example of mastery of the texture of wood as demonstrated in the design of the Virgin's cloak. Photograph, courtesy of the Metropolitan Museum of Art, New York City.

Fig. 40. "Mother and Child," by William Zorach (1927). Brazilian walnut. Collection of the artist.

Fig. 41. "Revenge," by Ernst Barlach (1928). 24½ inches high. Photograph, courtesy of the Buchholz Gallery, New York City.

Fig. 42. "Reclining Figure," by Henry Moore (1945-46). A masterly achievement in contemporary sculpture, and a superb integration of wood with design. The fluid, flowing shapes glide organically into the next shape, creating a movement as free as the flow of a wave. Courtesy of the Buchholz Gallery, New York City.

Fig. 43. "The Chief," by Constantin Brancusi (1923). Photograph, courtesy of the Buchholz Gallery, New York City.

Fig. 45. "Rooster." American folk art (Pennsylvania-German) by an unknown artist and the date unknown. 10½ inches high. In the collection of the Museum of Modern Art, New York City.

Fig. 44. "Totem Pole" of red cedar, by John and Fred Wallace (1939), both of whom are Haida Indians. On extended loan to the collection of the Museum of Modern Art, New York City, by the Indian Arts and Crafts Board of the U. S. Department of the Interior.

Fig. 46. "Bieri," a Gabun head, an example of African woodcarving. Date unknown. From Haut O'Gue, French Africa. In the collection of Mme. Helena Rubinstein.

Fig. 48. "Figure," French, Africa. Date unknown. Possibly a commemorative figure. In the collection of Chaim Gross. Photographer, Soicho Sunami.

Fig. 47. "Figure," Cameroon, African Negro, Gabun. From the collection of Miss Laura Harden, New York City. Photograph, courtesy of the Museum of Modern Art, New York City. Photographer, Walker Evans.

Fig. 49. "Scholar at Work,"
Ch'ing dynasty (1633-1912),
a statuette of wood, poly-
chromed. In the collection
of the Metropolitan Museum
of Art, New York City.

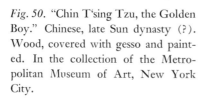

Fig. 50. "Chin T'sing Tzu, the Golden
Boy." Chinese, late Sun dynasty (?).
Wood, covered with gesso and paint-
ed. In the collection of the Metro-
politan Museum of Art, New York
City.

becomin
a sculpto
of wood

THE great revival of interest in wood for sculpture, after a long period of indifference, can be accounted for to a great extent by the uncovering of an adequate supply of a large variety of unusual woods with new and fascinating attributes.

New fields of expression have been opened for sculptors who understand and rejoice in the almost limitless possibilities lying hidden in these inert blocks of wood from which such marvelously beautiful effects can be won by the artist.

As more and more artists, both beginners and those with experience, turn their attention to this material which offers them fresh delights and challenges, many find they must feel their way slowly along in learning how to use a long neglected medium. It is my hope in this book to help shorten their apprenticeship and to reach more quickly the full enjoyment of carving wood with assurance and skill.

Because I am credited with having been instrumental in the

rn sculptors to the potentialities of this half
m, it is only fitting that I share with others the
use. If, while presenting technical methods, I can also
e idea of the satisfaction to be found in carving wood, the
f the book will have been realized.

WOOD SCULPTURE VS. WOOD CARVING

Wood carving, as such, is a very old activity, over five thousand years to be specific. Although there can be no wood sculpture without carving, still there is quite a gap between wood *carving* and wood *sculpture*. The difference, as I see it, is that much of the wood carving in the past was done to produce applied decoration and the principal appeal of a good deal of it in other forms was to astonish people into wondering how anyone could do such ingenious and intricate work.

To my mind, carving of that kind cannot be dignified with the term "sculpture." I do not, however, include in this statement the legion of examples of wood carving from all countries and periods that are truly sculptural.

All that I am going to say about how to carve so as to produce sculpture will, of course, be my own opinion founded on my own experience. I also hope no one will take every one of my explanations and recommendations as rigid rules of procedure, if they can devise better ones that will suit them and work out well.

Professional artists, I feel confident, do not need any such warning, but the beginner or amateur too should have something of his own to say and should wish, sooner or later, to say it in his own way. Each beginner or experimenter will want to work out his own variations of technique after trying my methods.

42

BOYHOOD IN A FOREST

My love of wood reaches back to my childhood. I was born in a small village in the Carpathian Mountains. This region was rich with extensive tracts of birch, fir and pine trees. In this deep forest my father carried on his lumber business. There I endlessly watched the processes of lumbering carried on from the felling of trees to the cutting of logs into lumber. How I enjoyed the delicious, pungent smell of newly cut wood. Every evening after the day's work our household was a busy one with the peasants carving religious ornaments, household objects and utensils as a form of relaxation. I recall in particular a friend of the family who carved unusual toys on his frequent visits. And a rare treat was the occasion of my brother's visits when he would show me his sketch books. I would sit among them and copy illustrations in the family's religious books. Summer days meant happy times in the surrounding forests or watching the magic circus that came to town once a year. The colorful circus decorations and performances of the acrobats made so deep an impression that it later greatly influenced my work.

AN EARLY LEANING TOWARD DRAWING

World War I found us in the city of Kolomyja — a fighting area — where all work was so disrupted that it was necessary to flee to Budapest. Here I was obliged to work at various occupations for which I was not fitted. But then I became a jeweler's apprentice. This gave me a chance to use my drawing ability, which was a fortunate start for me.

In 1919 I entered the competition sponsored by an art school that had just been started. Out of the four hundred and fifty entrants I was one of the thirty chosen to be admitted to the school. For the first time I learned to draw from the nude.

Unstable conditions made it necessary to close the art school. I decided then to return to my family, and despite many difficulties I arrived in Galicia. No employment was available, which left my days free for sketching everything that attracted me. One day my brother who had emigrated to America sent me the necessary papers which would admit me to the United States.

THE NEW HOME

I arrived in New York in 1921 where I immediately resumed my art studies at night at the Educational Alliance on East Broadway and at the Beaux Arts Institute of Design. At the Educational Alliance I became one of a group of young artists, many of whose names are now familiar to all who are interested in the arts.

ADVISED TO TRY SCULPTURE

Leo Jackinson, a student sculptor, who was a tragic loss to his friends when he was drowned two years later, was a tremendous help to me. When he saw some of my drawings he was struck with their three dimensional quality and urged me to try sculpture. It was an invaluable suggestion, for I soon realized that sculpture was the form of creative work that truly appealed to me.

In 1927 I decided it was time for me to break away and start carving by myself, since my ideas went beyond the traditional training and I felt it was time for me to try them. So I settled in an attic studio on 14th Street in New York.

It is my contention that the traditional training, which to me means becoming familiar with the structure of the human body and the effects of movement on it, is not a *starting* point for an aspiring artist but a *point of departure*.

44

During this period I began to teach wood carving at the Educational Alliance. I am still teaching at the Alliance as well as a class at the New School for Social Research and the Five Town Music and Art School in Woodmere, L. I. Thus I keep in touch with a variety of student viewpoints.

wood,
the re-discovered
medium

So far I have told of events and circumstances that worked together to make me a sculptor with a special interest in wood. There are other factors that have had definite effects on my attitude toward sculpture, especially toward carving wood.

One of the most positive of these factors is that I like wood. I like to carve it and to judge how the work is going by feeling the carved surface. There is a satisfaction and pleasure in the sense of touch that establishes an intimate affinity with the wood. It is also a primary reason why I never use power driven tools at any stage of a carving. The use of my hands and the customary hand tools maintains the close contact with the wood that I enjoy. Just as important to me is the action of the tools in contact with the wood's texture, which adds another exquisite pleasure to carving, and the fine color and grain which is exposed by the carving.

Fine wood carving reached a high development in Europe during the French Gothic period when so much of it was used to adorn churches, other religious edifices, palaces and mansions. It has had fluctuating periods of popularity since then.

This changing interest might be accounted for by the fact that people did not know how to preserve wood by means as simple as we know now. Lack of our present day knowledge meant that the only safe method they had, and which I believe they liked too, was to color their work with paint. Some such protective measure was especially necessary on ships' figureheads which had to withstand extreme exposure to all kinds of weather. But with the recently discovered woods of exceptional inherent beauty, we do not have to use an opaque coating to preserve them.

My interest in wood, implanted in me in the Galician forests, probably gave me a curiosity to know about as many woods as one could. This native curiosity is undoubtedly the reason why I am credited with beginning the tradition in this country of wood sculpture as a fine art.

THE DISCOVERY OF "NEW" WOODS

By the time I gave up my school training I had found there were lumber yards in New York that had fascinating woods whose names stirred my imagination . . . woods that I had never heard of and which had never been used for sculpture. They were surprisingly hard. They had been in demand for commercial and manufacturing purposes but I saw no reason why I should not try carving them.

I reasoned that, since these woods were in demand for fine veneers, the same qualities that created this demand might make them desirable for sculpture. I was delighted and excited to find that their density offered a challenge that was far more stimulating than that of the softer woods. This was because of their stubborn resistance to carving tools. They had the added virtues of new kinds of lovely, interesting grains and beautiful colors. These prop-

47

erties are, I believe, responsible in great part for the growing interest in wood sculpture.

EFFECTS OF WOOD ON A SCULPTOR

The medium of wood exerts a direct influence on a carver who creates a form. He has that form pretty well outlined for him by the material itself, assuming he respects the shape of the block he chooses. His design is bound to be long or tall rather than broad when he is working with a log. With stone, any kind of mass can be worked out. There are those who glue pieces of wood together to get a wide, as well as a long, dimension. To me this violates the nature of the material sculpturally. Some other medium might just as well be used, possibly to better effect.

Many fine examples of wood carving, which can be considered to be true sculpture, show that their carvers respected, and adhered to, the shape of the material. This is shown in the tall, slender religious figures of the European Gothic period, the figures carved by African artists and by the North American Indians who produced the totem poles. Such work constitutes a precedent that seems to me a good one to follow. The restriction in the medium, if you want to consider it one, has the virtue of being a strong influence on the design which makes for solid, compact sculptural forms.

THE REWARDS WOODS OFFER

There are rich compensations in two other characteristics of fine wood that go a long way to balance limitations of form. These inherent virtues are the grain and color that make many woods

48

desirable for sculpture. Just as stone has its physical beauties, so has wood. However, in wood the effects are much more pronounced and thus play their parts vividly in the finished work.

GRAIN

A skillful designer and carver can be well rewarded by making use of the lines of the grain of wood to trace and reveal the form. At times he may find unexpected irregularities in the vertical line of the grain. The most extreme instance is a pattern of concentric rings formed by a branch growing out of the trunk at that point and leaving its mark in a series of growth rings of its own which interrupt the vertical grain of the trunk. But instead of considering such irregularities as flaws or obstacles, the wood sculptor's ingenuity is challenged and exercised to adapt them interestingly and artistically into the design.

COLOR

Wood colors run the gamut from almost white through yellow, red and brown to velvety black. Some species are figured with a pattern, at times startling, of two or more colors. This allows the sculptor great freedom and variety for his ideas for subjects since with such variety, he can easily choose an appropriate color to enhance the effect of his work.

Lignum vitae presents a combination of colors that I have found particularly provocative. Around its black inner wood that comprises the greater part of a log, with possibly a pale brown running through it, there is an outer layer of light yellow, about an inch thick, on a log eight to ten inches in diameter. I have made use of both colors in a subject. There are also variations in shades of solid colored wood that lend interest to a carved surface.

49

Wood sculpture exists that has been given a finish of heavy wax, highly polished, which completely hides the original color of the wood. The effect is almost that of dark bronze. To me, that comes close to masking the color of the wood with paint.

HOW TO USE

WOOD'S ATTRIBUTES

With these rewarding elements to work with, the big question is how best to use them. It is not always easy to be sure whether an idea has demanded a specific block of wood or a piece of wood has suggested the idea. Sometimes however, there is no doubt how the decision was made; the wood obviously called forth the form. Suffice it to say, there must always be an harmonious relationship between the idea and the form of a specific piece of wood. Neither the idea nor the block should be tortured to make them merge.

In my work I make almost constant use of the human form. The reason is simple. It is a long form and can be carved from a cylindrical medium. And it provides a satisfactory arrangement of masses that can be manipulated to obtain endless different designs. If I carved a figure from wood and represented it naturalistically all I would have would be a figure in wood. But so much of the material would have been eliminated that I might as well have cast it in some other material. So I distort the forms of a body enough to keep them in the shape of the block so as to sacrifice a minimum amount of the wood. By leaving as much wood as possible I maintain the solidity of the medium.

This enables me to create an original sculptural form whose subject matter still is familiar to the observer. I try to restrict the composition so that the form I want to bring out of the wood is an easily comprehended unit. One of the ways of doing so is to avoid emphasizing parts of a body that might be distractions, such as an expression of a face or large breasts on a woman's figure, a device characteristic of Indian sculpture, or emphasis of the head by exaggerating its size, which is typical of Negro sculpture. In other words, I strive for a balanced design.

Negro sculpture does two things, among many others, which I find particularly admirable. For one, it shows that fine work can be done by judiciously combining abstract and representational elements and still keep to the basic tree trunk form. The other is the practice of confining the limbs of a subject in the cylindrical form so that they do not project outward from the vertical axis of the wood.

By not freeing them from the column of wood so that they are in a horizontal position, I maintain the nature of the medium. Projecting elements can be a distraction to the observer because of the vaguely disturbing feeling that they could so easily break off.

All this is not stated as a fixed rule. It is possible to have arms and legs free of the rest of the material but arranged to help achieve a flowing rhythmic design and still be harmonious with the mass so long as they do not project outward.

It is typical of Negro art that the figures are posed in several frontal positions but without giving any impression of being static. I prefer to give my figures what I regard as a more pleasing feeling. This makes them interesting to the observer through a suggestion of a rising, spiral movement, by arranging the feet, hips and head so that each points in a slightly different direction. This creates a pleasant ascending line that carries the eye upward.

I was brought up to rejoice in God and life and to have a gay and festive spirit. Giving way to despondency was frowned upon and discouraged. This attitude is not necessarily consciously applied to my work but, from the comments often made that many of my sculptures convey a feeling of gaiety and humor, I am sure it is embodied in it.

SUMMARY OF MY APPROACH
TO CARVING SCULPTURE IN WOOD

My approach to wood sculpture is that work done in this medium should convey the feeling of the density and weight of wood and reveal its intrinsic beauty in sculptural form. I believe a work of art should appeal to the higher instincts of man and bring him pleasure and contentment. It should stir the observer's imagination and awaken in him a consciousness of significant form hitherto unknown to him.

I feel that I reach a larger audience by generalizing my figures severely so that the spectator can relate himself to them without undue interference from the sculptor's detailed conception. This is achieved to a great extent by planned and considered distortion and my own version of stylization to heighten the aesthetic effectiveness of my work and give it life.

wood

THE first essential element you must have to carve a piece of wood sculpture is, of course, a suitable piece or block of wood. The word block is a convenient one to use when speaking of a short, chunky piece of log in contrast to an elongated piece of log or a long slab.

If you are in a large center, such as New York, check the lumber yards until you find one with a good supply of interesting woods in stock. You will probably find there is usable mahogany and walnut available wherever you are as they are stocked in many parts of the country. If I had not lived in New York City when I began my career as a sculptor I might not yet have discovered the exceptional and, up to then, unfamiliar woods that have made wood sculpture as varied and exciting as it is today.

DISCOVERY OF EXOTIC HARDWOODS

After working in class with the softer woods, usual and wise for the novice wood carver to start on, I investigated the lumber yards that were then in the lower part of Manhattan. I began to hear about woods with alluring names that grow in the West Indies and Central and South America and asked to see them. That was the beginning of my education in the exotic hardwoods. It took little time to realize that interesting and attractive hardwoods, appropriate for sculpture, are imported from all parts of the world, especially the East Indies, Africa, Turkey, the Philippines and other distant countries. A great number are described and commented on in detail in the Appendix on Wood in the back of this book.

I experimented and discovered infinite pleasure and a greater thrill out of carving the harder woods. The first satisfaction was the sturdy resistance of the wood to the cutting tools and the next one was the magnificent color revealed by the process of cutting.

FAVORITE WOODS

In time, out of fifty varieties, I have come to prefer lignum vitae which grows in the West Indies and Central America, the hardest wood known, velvet black in tone; snakewood from Dutch Guiana in northern South America, hard and reddish brown with brown and black spots as they might appear in a snakeskin; ebonies which grow in Ceylon, the Dutch East Indies and South America, in shades of red, green and purple blacks; greenheart wood from South America, pale yellow-green to black; cocobolo from Central America, reddish in color with subtle and varied grain patterns; beefwood from British Guiana on the northern coast of South America, dark in color with a crossgrain that resembles the pattern of the grain of beef; and some of the rosewoods which are found in Brazil, the East Indies, Honduras and Madagascar, that vary in color and have a fine striped grain.

Lignum vitae is my first choice because its extreme density gives me the greatest carving satisfaction I have ever experienced.

If I can find as many favorites as I have commented on above you can do the same out of the hundred or more species that are

54

appropriate for sculpture. This ample supply includes woods softer than those I have listed, which some sculptors may prefer over the extremely hard varieties.

WHERE TO ACQUIRE
INTERESTING WOOD

The fact that a sculptor is not near to a good source of supply of these special choice woods need not be a matter for great concern for he can quite readily get in touch with yards that do handle them. However, I do not advise the beginner in wood sculpture to use these woods until he has carved mahogany and walnut which can be obtained more easily. They are softer varieties than I like, but they are by no means the softest and their characteristics are excellent for developing your carving technique. At the same time, they possess good color and grain so that pieces worked from them will reflect their natural beauty.

There are ways to collect logs and blocks nearly anywhere if a lumber yard is not convenient to you, or if the local yard is short on wood adaptable for carving. Should you hear of anyone cutting down some apple, cherry or pear trees you have right at hand a source of useful carvable wood. Go and see it and if it looks interesting you can acquire some of it and arrange to have it cut in lengths which you can transport and store conveniently.

Of course, you must avoid decayed wood, but if the center part is in poor condition yet the rest of it is thick enough to give it strength and rigidity, the wood can be used. You can either ream out the soft part or bore a hole in short sections which will rid you of the poor wood and at the same time expose more surface inside in order to speed up the process of drying.

I once carved a head from just such a piece. I simplified the removal of the soft inside by cutting a lengthwise panel out of one side from top to bottom. The rest of the block still had plenty of surface to carve. Its only drawback was it was better if it was placed in a position where the open cut wasn't readily seen.

HOW TO PROTECT
YOUR WOOD SUPPLY

When you get your wood to where it is going to be stored for seasoning, strip off the bark and heavily shellac the ends of each piece, applying three or four coats. This prevents cracks starting at the ends, which they are inclined to do.

Then store the wood in a barn, shed or cellar. Don't fail to raise it from the ground or floor so that air can circulate all around it. Be sure also that the storage place will always be dry and cool. If you maintain these conditions, in two years you will have wood seasoned well enough for carving.

Other perfectly good sources of wood are timbers and other large wood elements from an old building that is being torn down, as well as pieces of old furniture which have some large elements in them. Such wood is seasoned but until you use it, store it where it will not be able to absorb moisture.

For a long time I have kept wood on hand in my studio, some of which has been there as long as fifteen years. The room has an iron, wood-burning stove which takes off the chill of the air in extreme cold weather and which can quickly do away with any excessive collection of moisture.

My logs and blocks, lying on blocks or cleats, are becoming more than merely well seasoned . . . their state is ideal!

A practice to follow scrupulously is to keep wood away from

all direct sources of heat such as hot pipes, a stove, a furnace or exposure to direct sunlight. It is important to remember that concentrated heat dries the wood too fast. This condition causes it to develop splits and cracks. Wood can be stored outdoors if air circulates around it and it is shielded from rain and sun but it will probably take longer to season than if it were in a dry, cool enclosed location. The enemies of felled wood are moisture, humidity, pronounced changes of temperature, insects and fungi. The conditions to be observed in storage reduce the chances of these enemies attacking the material.

HOW WOOD IS SEASONED

Like so many processes of nature, the seasoning of wood takes place very deliberately. An idea of the rate can be gathered from the fact that it takes a plank one inch thick a year to dry properly. All woods do not season at the same rate. Very hard woods, such as lignum vitae, snakewood and ebony, take longer, for example, than softer varieties such as mahogany and walnut. The greatest stress in the wood as it dries is across the grain and only very little with the grain.

Dealers in logs and blocks of sculptors' woods have devised a simple method of arriving at seasoned wood more quickly than if it were left in the form of a log. The structure of the wood makes this possible.

The bulk of a tree trunk, the usable wood, is called the heartwood. It is surrounded by an outer layer, the sapwood. This is the part that provides expansion of the trunk a little each year by changing into heartwood. Each year of growth can be detected in a cross section of a log as one ring in the pattern of concentric rings called "growth rings." The familiar outer covering of the sapwood is the bark.

The very center of the heartwood is the "pith" and the wood immediately surrounding it is spoken of as the heart of the heartwood. It cannot be delimited in an exact way as it varies with the age and condition of the tree. As wood seasons, the heart and pith necessarily dry more slowly than any other part of a log. Many lumbermen believe it never dries as much as the rest of the heartwood does and is, thus, a constant hazard as a possible cause of checking or splitting.

A way to eliminate this uncertainty in a thick log is to cut it up lengthwise into long parts and then cut the heart away from them wherever it is still attached. The plan by which a log is cut to accomplish this is well thought out in advance to provide the maximum number of useful pieces. Obviously, they are not as thick as the uncut log was and will, therefore, season in less time than the log would have.

The pith of the heartwood is not always in the geometrical center of a tree trunk. Sometimes it is well off center due to abnormal or unusual conditions during the tree's growth. It can be identified on a cross section of a log as the part made up of the minute inner growth rings.

A test as to whether a log or block is reasonably sound is to strike it with the knuckles or some hard object. If it gives off a kind of ringing tone it is probably in proper condition. A dull, dead sound is a sign of a crack, a hollowness or dampness.

COMMERCIAL FACTS
ABOUT SCULPTORS' WOODS

Sooner or later you will run across some lumbermens' terms with which you should be familiar. To people in the wood business logs don't crack or split. They check. And a piece cut from a log isn't just a piece. It's a flitch. Webster's definition for it is "An outside piece cut from a tree trunk."

Flitches that have had the heartwood sliced off are in the form of polyhedrons. That is to say, they range from long to stubby columns of wood with squared-off ends and several side surfaces which are roughly rectangular planes of different widths.

Dealers in the exceptional woods point out that logs and blocks suitable for carving are by no means "scrap." They are, on the contrary, a by-product of logs which are usually sliced up for veneers. In the process of cutting veneers there is a limitation as to the length of log that can be fitted onto a slicing machine. The parts that have to be cut off to make them fit can then be cut into small pieces for other commercial uses or they are made available for sculptors. Yards are making better use of this wood than they did when I first became interested in it; in those days they were often surprised at the pieces I considered possible for sculpture.

Companies that have the rare pieces advertise in periodicals reaching sculptors and sculpture students. One organization I know well issues a comprehensive list which describes the stock clearly, giving dimensions of each log and block. Short of going to the yard, to study and order from such a list is a practical way of obtaining interesting pieces.

PRICES

The prices in the list prove that wood sculpture is far from an extravagant activity. Blocks range from $1.20 for a 4 x 4 x 11 inch piece of African mahogany to $160.00 for a 22 x 27 x 27 inch piece of Bubinga, African rosewood. Comparatively few of the nearly 500 items are priced over $50.00.

There are logs available from 3 to 12 feet long and 5 to 18 inches in diameter which are sold by weight. Lignum vitae logs, weighing from 60 to 120 pounds, 5 to 18 inches in diameter and 3 to 6 feet long, sell at 10¢ a pound for the whole log or 20¢ a pound for pieces, while ebony, the most expensive wood listed, is available in logs from 60 to 120 pounds, 5 to 18 inches in diameter and 3 to 4 feet long, and is quoted at 30¢ a pound for full length logs and 60¢ a pound for pieces. A buyer can be sure that all this wood has been seasoned slowly by the natural process with no artificial assistance.

LIFE EXPECTANCY
OF FELLED WOOD

A carved piece of wood can remain intact indefinitely, as is proved by the oldest Egyptian sculptures seen in museums, which are still in sound condition. To be sure, they had a particularly good start in life because of Egypt's climate, but with proper care, today's wood sculpture can be so treated as to last indefinitely. This will be gone into in some detail when we discuss the subject of the final finish applied to a carving.

So much for the essential elements of wood sculpture. Let's move on to the other elements required to transform a portion of a tree trunk into a new and significant form.

the workroom
and equipment

A wood sculptor demands and requires less of a studio or workroom than does a painter. North light is good but not a necessity. A good deal of work can be done under artificial light and the posing of a model can be done somewhere else if the studio light isn't right. An actual working space of 12 by 12 feet is adequate, and a ceiling high enough for a long piece of wood to stand upright comfortably is essential.

An imperative condition is the ability to maintain the air in a cool, dry state. Since too much heat and moisture causes cracks to open in wood with a weathered outside surface, it is obvious that when that surface is being cut away by carving the wood is even more vulnerable to unfavorable conditions.

SIZE OF WORKING SPACE

Wood sculptures tend to be of modest size but it is certainly not true of all of them. I have several large subjects in the studio —

one, for instance, is about three feet wide and six feet high. This I was able to carve in a limited space with no particular inconvenience. A good deal of the work was done with the block — a large, slab-like piece of the trunk of a mahogany tree — lying on the floor. At other times I propped it up against the work bench, if that gave me a better working position.

This leads into an interesting side issue that is worth attention. As the subject done from this large block was wide but not very thick, to follow the design meant that I had to remove good-sized pieces before I began carving. I planned how I could saw them out so that I would have useful blocks for other subjects. It is, perhaps, a minor point, but by using forethought and imagination one can sometimes salvage pieces which otherwise would simply be discarded.

THE WORK BENCH

A large bench is not a necessity. I have done all my work on a carpenter's bench 32 inches high with a top area 20 inches wide and 44 inches long. It is equipped with a wooden vise, which I use occasionally, but its principal value is for use as a table or platform on which to lay a carving at a convenient height to work on. Or, I can prop the piece I am working on up against it when I reach the stage of smoothing the surfaces.

HOW TO STEADY A BLOCK

Large and bulky pieces of wood stand or lie solidly of their own weight. But if you want to do a small carving the best way to hold it firmly in a good working position is to put it in a vise attached to

62

your work bench. The vise can be either the carpenter's wooden type or of the all-metal kind called a machinist's vise. It is not necessary to have any pad between the wood being carved and the jaws of a carpenter's vise as the wooden jaws don't bite into the wood. But the jaws of a metal vise can leave a squeeze mark unless some kind of shield is provided to be adjusted each time you change the position of the block or fitted over the jaws permanently. The best material for pads or covers is calf skin.

A useful piece of equipment for carving a bulky block is a stand about two feet high with a stationary or revolving platform a foot and a half to two feet square.

Another way of stabilizing a block is to screw it to a base of some kind, then clamp or screw that base to the bench or stand. This, however, has the drawback of limiting you to only one position and allowing no freedom to lay the block on its sides in different positions for convenience in carving.

The vise, as I said above, is useful principally for carving small pieces. I want to sound a serious word of caution about holding a piece of wood in one hand while carving with the other. *Never do it!* Even when the cutter is not as sharp as it should be. Ugly wounds have resulted from being careless about this.

TOOLS

Tools are grouped in four categories. They are mallets, cutters, sharpeners and abraders. A few additional simple materials round out the list of equipment.

For anyone learning wood sculpture one mallet is enough. Only three sizes are carried by dealers and a full set is not necessary at first. The cutters consist of gouges and flat chisels. Sharpeners are used continually. Abraders — the smoothers and scrapers — are

63

rasps, rifflers (special kinds of small rasps), scrapers and sandpaper. The finishing materials are white shellac, alcohol, olive oil, fine steel wool, a good floor wax and soft cloths.

A typical set to start with is (Fig. 7):

MALLET: 1 — 18 oz., which will be 18 inches long turned either in one piece or with head and handle fitted together.

CUTTERS: 3 gouges — 1 each: ⅛ inch, ⅝ inch and 1 inch wide. 1 fishtail gouge ¾ inch wide.

SHARPENERS: 1 India special gouge slip; 2 small slips. 1 bench oilstone.

ABRADERS:

Wood rasps: 1 each 6 inches and 8 inches long. 1 rounded on one side and flat on the other, 6 inches long. 3 steel scrapers, 1 with straight edge, 2 with rounded edges.

FINISHING MATERIALS: As stated above.

All of these pieces of equipment will be commented on presently. To give you an idea of the basic equipment you will probably want when you have mastered the rudiments of carving, I have listed my own essential equipment in the Appendix on Tools.

In addition to the cutters suggested here, there are five other kinds for special purposes, the need for which you will learn after some experience, if you decide you need them at all. They are spoon and fishtail flat chisels, and spoon, fishtail, bent-back and long-bent gouges. Some of these are for deep cutting of which I do practically none. Your own experience will determine for you whether or not you need any of these specialized tools.

MALLETS

Mallet woods vary in weight from lignum vitae, the heaviest, to beech and then hickory. A mallet really has two weights and can be held by the head instead of the handle. This hand grasp makes it possible to deliver a lighter blow than the greater momentum the head has when it is swung at the end of the handle. The last gouges used in the cutting process, the narrow ones, are impelled merely by a light blow of your fist or the palm of your hand.

WHY GOUGES CUT

Since 1912 it has been conceded that English steel is the best material for wood carving tools. It is choice, well-tempered and properly hardened.

The general term for a gouge is "chisel" but since the blade is concave it is called a gouge, which describes its cutting action, that of scooping. This concave blade forms a curved cutting edge in the shape of an arc varying from almost flat to semicircular. Some gouges are shaped to cut deeper than just a semicircle would allow by having the ends of the arc slightly extended. This makes it cut a deeper groove, elliptical in form. The gouge is almost the only type of cutter I use as it removes wood cleanly and precisely when cutting across the grain and the variation in shape from deep to almost flat does all the kinds of cutting I require.

A gouge cuts because the end of the blade is ground at a bevel on its under side. When ground, this is a shiny surface one-half to three-quarters of an inch wide and provides an edge which can be made very keen by further sharpening on fine grain stones.

DISCOVERY ABOUT BEVELS
FOR CUTTING EDGES

The angle of the bevel should be varied, as I discovered, for different wood densities. Hardwoods require a bevel at a little greater angle to the upper surface of the blade than soft woods do. You become familiar with the proper angle after you have used the tools awhile. When you buy gouges from a dealer the first grinding will have been done but not all dealers realize that the variation in the angle of the bevel is important. You have to specify whether you want a chisel ground for hard or soft wood.

Dealers say that the bevel should be ground to as flat a surface as possible. My experience inclines me to the conviction that a slightly rounded, or bulging, surface — that is, not the cutting edge of a gouge but the area of the bevel — is stronger than an absolutely flat one.

FLAT CHISELS

I make no use of flat chisels . . . the familiar carpenter's tool. They are useful for carving furniture decoration or for some deep cutting. Since I prefer rounded surfaces that don't sink deep into the mass of the wood at any point and since I carve across the grain I can dispense with flat chisels. In fact cross-grain cutting with flat chisels, which cut well *with* the grain, would be disastrous as they tear the wood on each side of the chisel instead of taking it away cleanly. However, because flat chisels may be used at times I will comment on them.

Their cutting edges are at a right angle to the parallel sides of the blade and they are useful for taking off wood readily with the grain. A skew chisel is flat but the cutting edge is ground at a 45 degree angle with the sides of the blade. This forms a point at the end of the longest side, a form which is useful for careful shaving of a surface and the point, of course, can get into deep depressions, if necessary.

SPECIAL CUTTERS

Other cutters are simply variations of flat chisels and gouges, as their names indicate. The bent chisels are for deep cutting, and the fishtail chisel, so named because the cutting edge is wide and tapers quickly to a thin shank, is valuable for careful smoothing of a surface.

Chisels remove wood in shavings and chips. The wider the blade the bigger the chip. The narrowest blades remove little chips as thin as shavings. It is not possible to produce a satin smooth surface with chisels, especially gouges.

Chisels come in hundreds of shapes and sizes. Considering their high quality, their prices are reasonable. Straight gouges, the type of cutter I use almost exclusively, are priced from $2.75 to $3.75, and flat chisels a little less. The most expensive, a 1½ inch wide fishtail gouge, costs $4.50. Handles are 25¢. Mallets sell for approximately $5.00. Dealers in tools can be located through advertisements of sculptor's equipment.

ABRADERS FOR SMOOTHING

The slightly uneven marks left by the narrowest and flattest gouges are removed by the abraders . . . the rasps, rifflers, scrapers and sandpaper . . . all obtainable in well-stocked hardware stores. I will explain how you can make your own scrapers when we describe the part of the process where they are used.

67

WHY, WHEN AND HOW
TO KEEP CHISELS SHARP

Sharpeners are essential equipment and the technique of using them is an essential skill that must be learned. How to sharpen the cutting tools requires a somewhat technical and detailed explanation which, if taken up here, would delay our getting to the process of carving. It is therefore thoroughly described in the Appendix on Sharpeners.

There are good and sound reasons why a keen edge must constantly be maintained on all the cutting tools as you use them.

Poor cutting edges are those that are not keen and also those with nicks in them. A properly sharp edge can be maintained on a gouge by rocking the bevel with slow careful motions on a bench or oilstone. Next, a new form of sharpener called an India special gouge slip can be used or the final whetting can take place on the small India carving tool slip.

The special gouge slip is about five inches long and is a slender cone with about one-third of its mass hollowed out. This provides a concave surface and the rest of the cone form affords a convex area that fits all variations of gouge widths and depths.

You keep one of the small slips right at hand at all times and rub it frequently, with some pressure, along the cutting edge.

If the chisel develops small nicks grind it down with a small rotary grindstone or on a bench oilstone. Then whet it with the special slip, if you have one, and next with the small one. If a nick is too large to respond readily to that treatment the chisel must be taken to a professional grinder who has a large rotary grindstone, probably power-operated, which will grind away enough metal to eliminate the nick and produce a new bevel for a fresh start. A nicked cutting edge can harm a surface, especially on soft wood, by leaving traces in the form of ridges.

68

Perhaps the best reason for sharp tools is the satisfaction they contribute to the carving process. Really keen edges make carving a pleasure, whereas, to work with dull ones means hard, unsatisfactory and sometimes exasperating labor. Sharp tools give the feeling that you are a much better carver than you are when you struggle along with dull cutters. When the tools respond so amiably to your guidance, you are assured of smooth progress.

With this introduction to the tools you use to carve with we are now ready to take the step. What have you decided to carve?

the idea and
the block

THE idea of what you want to carve has taken form in your mind, and if you have a supply of wood you have probably decided what kind of wood you will use and what its mass is to be. Or, you may have only the idea and you now go in search of the wood. Searching will probably demonstrate to you that it is more satisfactory to have a stock of wood of your own on hand as it gives you more time to mull over the relation between the idea and the wood.

Finally you select the block (Figs. 1 and 2) whose soundness you determine first by striking it and hearing a healthy ringing sound. You already know the color of the wood because when you initially acquired the block you sliced a bit off the weathered surface with a knife or shallow sampling gouge. Now is the time to make several other sampling cuts to find out if the color varies in different parts of the block.

As I have said before, sometimes the idea determines the wood you will use, and vice versa. It is often hard to know which came first.

HOW TO STUDY THE BLOCK

Either way, you put the selected block under observation and study. Most of your acquaintance with it, before carving, can be made by becoming familiar with the grain, how it looks and what it seems to do, judging by what it reveals of itself at each squared-off end. It can tell you by the growth rings if there is heartwood or if it has been cut away, and how the rings are arranged in the flitch. Different patterns of rings at each end mean the direction of the grain changes somewhere in its length.

If you expect to make use of the grain to emphasize a swelling form you will want to decide on which side of the piece this can be accomplished best. That will have a good deal to do with which side will be the front view.

When you carve away wood which has pronounced lines of grain, it is apparent that if you cut across the lines at the right point at an angle, a round or conical form that projects from the surface will have lines of grain going around it describing a pattern of concentric circles.

Suggestions of this kind are made merely as examples of how you can look for the particularities of a block from which you can make deductions as to its composition and patterns. As much as I would like to do so there is no way I know of to tell you how to judge in advance the concealed characteristics of a piece of carvable wood. That ability comes only by working with a large variety of species and many pieces of wood.

Even the ringing sound test can be deceptive. In spite of a good sound you may still come across an internal crack, or a condition which I call a sandpocket. That means a hollow in the wood where sand or dirt has accumulated. It can be caused by a small branch, probably a low one, breaking off or shed by the tree. Its core softens and crumbles away in minute quantities before being covered by the slow process of growth of the wood. But meanwhile dirt has probably lodged within the wood. Another cause is where there has been roughness, such as wrinkled wood in a branch crotch. This is bound to collect waste which is overgrown and would never be seen again until the wood is cut into.

HOW THE BLOCK INFLUENCES
THE FINISHED WORK

Considerations such as these mean that the block's inner, as well as outer, characteristics influence the form and appearance of your finished subject. Dense and tough woods can be fashioned in beautiful masses that will take fine detail. You will have decided whether the finished work is to have a smooth and polished surface or be rough and rugged. If it is not to be smooth an effect can be achieved by leaving an area of deep or shallow gouge marks. Or, some areas will perhaps show cutter marks and others will be smooth, for purposes of contrast, or to indicate texture, such as drapery or clothing next to flesh.

THE TWO OR THREE
DIMENSIONAL SKETCH

Now we are at the point where you have to make a record of some kind to guide your carving. Before you work with a living model, if the idea requires one, it's a good idea to do some sketching to see how the idea shapes up in graphic form. By experience you will determine whether you prefer to have a rough clay model as your guide, or whether a drawing is sufficient for you. A clay figure may appeal to you because it is a guide in the rough.

My preference is for a drawing (Figs. 3, 4 and 5). I take plenty of time and make several until I am satisfied with it as a sketch. The final one I sometimes render in wash or soft pencil to give it a three dimensional aspect. Sometimes I finish it in pen and ink or water color. It is just as well to have the working drawing as near as possible to the size of the subject you are going to carve.

PLACING CUTTING LIMIT LINES
ON THE BLOCK

This is useful because the next step is to take the drawing in hand and indicate its outline and main features in broad lines right on the wood (Fig. 9). If the drawing is full size its lines can be transferred directly to the wood without changing the scale. Putting lines on the block can also be done by standing a clay model next to it and indicating the design on it, as is done from a drawing with chalk, charcoal or lead paint. The lines you put on the block are going to be your guide in chipping away surplus wood.

Do not be surprised that the appearance of the object as you carve turns out to be somewhat different from the sketch. The model or drawing is bound to look much freer than the subject as it emerges from the hard medium. This is natural because of the wood's resistance to the cutting tool, which after all, is not a pencil racing over paper.

The design of the subject will determine for you how many views need to be drawn. If all views are very different you will need drawings for each of them. If it is simply a woman's head with a mass of hair falling to the base of the block at the back you could conceivably get along with only a front and a side view as the form of the hair can be modelled by eye as you progress.

the emergence
of your idea
from the block

Now, with the block resting on a stand or held in a vise, and the gouge sharpened, you are ready to start to carve (Fig. 10).

The edge along the squared-off top of the block nearly always has to be eliminated so that this is a good place to start. If it is a large block you wrestle it around and lay it on its side until the edge you want to start cutting is uppermost. If it wobbles at all put some kind of a wedge under it at the strategic place or places. You have selected the uppermost edge because that is the most convenient position. It is a comfortable, accessible working position which gives you full control of the tools.

HOW YOU USE
THE FIRST CUTTING TOOL

Since the first cutting you do is not precision work you use as large a gouge as the situation allows (Figs. 10, 11 and 12). For instance, a deep inch-wide tool is appropriate for a block two feet

74

high. A larger block could take a wider gouge and, conversely, a smaller block a narrower one. Some use a straight chisel at this point but, as I said before, it will tear the wood away rather than cut it. A deep gouge removes the wood in large chips whose mass is about that of a golf ball but the shape is flatter, of course.

The gouge is grasped firmly with the left hand, if you are right-handed, well down the handle leaving two inches of handle exposed (Fig. 14). This gives good control for guiding the tool and placing it at the starting point of each new cutting path, as well as serving to prevent striking your hand with the mallet.

Pick up your heaviest mallet by the handle and place the gouge at a 45 degree angle to the wood so that it will cut across the grain. Then begin a steady series of three strong blows with the mallet. The first blow sinks the gouge into the wood. Then depress the handle and strike it. This drives the gouge forward. On the third blow give the gouge an upward scooping pressure. This will remove the chip.

The thickness of the blade acts as a sharp wedge and loosens large chips because you are making deep, liberal cuts that are producing a comparatively smooth trough. When you come to the end of the path, the edge of the wood, lever the gouge forward to get rid of the last chip. Then look to see that you are not cutting too near the guide line. As you will progress from medium wide to narrow gouges during the rest of the cutting, you approach gradually the surface of the subject you are bringing out of the wood.

To learn to do this kind of chipping well, without spoiling a good block, I advise doing a good deal of it on a bulky piece of wood, preferably of the kind you are going to carve, which you can afford to sacrifice in practice. What you must learn is to keep cutting chips steadily of about the same size. If they vary noticeably it means that either your mallet's blows are not all of equal power or you are not guiding the gouge steadily.

When you can guide a cutter so that it makes a straight path several inches long which is practically the same depth from end to end you have learned how to synchronize your mallet blows with the gouge and how to guide it.

Now that the first path is cut, go back to where it was started and begin to cut another path next to it. This will leave a sharp dividing ridge between them. Continue to do this until all the area you can remove comfortably, with the block in the first position, is cut away.

EYE PROTECTORS

If, during this operation, chips jump about so that your eyes wince, it is time to wear goggles (Fig. 10) or one of the transparent plastic working hoods, suggestive of the headgear worn by welders. These can be obtained in sculptor's supply stores or through their catalogues. It is poor judgment to expect to work well when you are distracted by flying chips. And, who wants to get a dangerous splinter in his eye? Small chips made by the medium narrow gouges can be more annoying than large chips.

HOW YOU USE
THE SECOND CUTTING TOOL

When the first area you can work on efficiently has been cut over, shift the block to another comfortable position and remove an area of wood just as you did the first one. Repeat this until all areas to be carved have had the first layer of wood removed. But keep checking the guide lines to be sure you are not cutting too near them. They should be approached gradually.

76

When you clear the floor after the first cutting do not throw out all the chips. Select the large ones from different areas of the block, if there is a noticeable variation in color, to use for mending if a crack or split should develop in the piece at any time. How to make use of them is explained later.

By the time you have cut away all the wood you think is advisable with the widest gouge, you will have the satisfaction of seeing the general form of the subject revealed enough to be recognizable (Fig. 15). That is, if you have been seeing the form in your mind as you have been cutting. The guide lines can not tell you exactly how far to approach them and how deep to cut to in some places. This is a matter of judgment.

At this stage the block will be covered with several areas of gouge marks, each area and group with a pattern of marks going in a different direction from its neighbor.

If this phase of the work seems slow and laborious to you at first, just remember the old carpenters' and wood carvers' adage to the effect that if you proceed circumspectly and with due caution you can always cut away just enough wood, but *you can never put chips back.*

THE PROGRESSION TO NARROWER
AND NARROWER GOUGES

At this point you are well into the project. Now you are ready to start using the cutters that will carry on the progression from a rough surface to a form that pretty well defines your ultimate idea. Now go over the entire carved surface with a narrower and flatter gouge (Fig. 13), chipping more carefully than with the first one and striking it only two or three times along a short path.

You held the first gouge at an angle of about 45 degrees to the

77

wood. From now on lessen that angle with each gouge, which is narrower with each change, until you are taking off small chips at the end of the cutting operations. Hold the gouge almost parallel with the wood.

Just exactly what angle you use to carve with each change of tool is determined by how much wood you want to remove and how the tool feels as you guide it. The obvious rule is, the larger the angle the bigger the chip.

There can, of course, be no set rule of procedure as to using only one width of gouge for each layer you take off. It is a matter of judgment depending on the conditions. What you do with the second gouge is to cut away the ridges between the rough paths and go down a little deeper. By selecting a narrower and flatter gouge each time you go over the surface of the block, you will be removing less and less wood each time and working toward a smoother surface.

DISAPPEARANCE OF ROUGH SKETCH LINES
FROM THE BLOCK

At some point, dictated by the situation, you have to chip away your drawing guide lines because they are on the outside surface of the block. When they have gone (Fig. 12) you know you are approaching the end of eliminating a liberal amount of surplus wood. Now you are, so to speak, for the first time face to face with the form you have in mind, as it is being evolved through, and influenced by, the medium you selected for the visualization . . . the wood.

Before you are through using the wider cutters you will probably be holding the mallet by the head or using a light mallet. When you use the narrow, shallow gouges you will put the mallet aside and strike the gouge with your fist or the palm of your hand. When you feel you have done all you can with a gouge you may be surprised to find how smooth the surface has become.

THE FIGURE HAS EMERGED

When you reach the point where you can see that even the narrowest and flattest gouge will take away too much wood (Fig. 17), the form of your sculptural idea should be complete and the details, such as eye sockets and lids, nose, lips and chin, should be well defined. To achieve this you have gone over the surface several times and have moved the block around as many times as necessary to put it in a good working position, even standing it on its head in order to bring out a feature such as the under side of the chin. In order to take off any more of the surface you must now abrade it instead of cut it.

using the abraders

THIS means you will next use the coarsest rasp (Figs. 18 and 19). But before applying it for the first time try it out on a piece of the same kind of wood you are carving which has been chipped to a well-smoothed surface. Rasps become dull and can make a mark on the wood instead of grating it. A rasp that is too worn had better be discarded or put aside to use when it can do no harm. To start the abrading process use a new rasp or one still in good condition.

Whether or not you use a rasp that is rounded on one side depends a good deal on the form of the surface you decide to grate. Only experience will tell you what each kind does. You use the flat and rounded side interchangeably. A coarse rasp leaves a fairly smooth, but not satin-smooth, surface.

With the abraders you follow the same kind of progression as you do with the cutters. You proceed from coarse to fine.

Make it a point to collect and save some of the wood dust while you are using the abraders. It will be useful if you want to fill a crack that is only a narrow fissure.

HOW TO USE A RASP

A rasp is employed a good deal of the time by holding the handle in one hand and applying pressure to the end of the blade with one or two fingers of the other hand at the end of the blade, except when you hold it just by the handle to get into concave surfaces, such as occur in the features of a face. Too much pressure on this sharp scraper can make marks that go below the surface you plan to have. You, of course, go over with the rasp every bit of surface that is to be smooth in the finished piece.

A very coarse rasp, naturally, removes wood faster than a finer one. You use it to take down a surface you have left quite rough on purpose because, in the design, it is supposed to be rougher than the very smooth areas.

My equipment includes rasps of different degrees of roughness to be used as the occasion demands. You can manipulate small ones without a handle. A slender, small round one comes in handy at times.

The rasps create a surface which will inform even a lay observer that the work is well advanced. Now the grain is also beginning to be seen readily.

RIFFLERS, AND HOW YOU USE THEM

The next kind of tool you use are the rifflers. They are all-metal and consist of a bar, serving as the handle, that joins together the ends shaped into a straight or bent point, flattish or round tools, with fine rasp scorings. Their function is to give sharp, clean definition by getting to the bottom of a fold or depression, such as the crease between the lips or into the modelling that forms an eyelid.

81

SCRAPERS FOR REMOVING IRREGULARITIES
LEFT BY OTHER TOOLS

After using the rasps and rifflers to accomplish all the results they are capable of, you are ready to begin the final smoothing, the operation which will give a skin-smooth surface where it is desired. The first stage of this operation is done with a scraper (Fig. 20). Hardware stores sell a wood scraping tool which is adequate. A spoke shave is also suggested in catalogues but I have never favored it. It is not useful for all surfaces and it is difficult to keep it from shaving off too much wood.

The most satisfactory form of scraper I have found is the edge of a thin plate of steel, roughly three by four inches in size. Given the piece of steel, which is not hard to come by, anyone can convert it into a scraper by rubbing the edge that forms the thickness of the plate with another piece of hard metal . . . a gouge shank for example, or a bench oilstone, using plenty of pressure against the edge so as to produce a miniscule burr, called a wire edge, spoken of in the Appendix on Sharpeners. This edge I consider ideal for smoothing a wood surface. I have scrapers for large, small and curved areas which are readily purchasable in stores.

An edge of a cleanly-cut piece of glass is a good scraper but it hasn't the permanence of a steel plate.

HOW TO HANDLE A SCRAPER

A scraper is used by holding it at a right angle to the wood between two fingers of each hand at the top corners. Scrape by pulling the tool toward you with the top edge leading the scraping edge. Or, it can be pushed away from you. Scrape in short motions and in all directions, with a gentle pressure, determined by the result the scraper is getting. Use the corners of the blade in depressions. And shift the block as often as necessary to get at each area comfortably.

Your patience is being well rewarded now as this operation brings out the color of the wood as the rasps brought out the grain.

SANDPAPER PRODUCES
A SKIN-SMOOTH SURFACE

The last operation of the raw wood is sandpapering. Have a good supply of sandpaper on hand with a variety of degrees of surface from coarse to fine.

Go all over the smooth area, sometimes with a piece of the sandpaper wrapped around your finger and at other times held flat. This produces an almost satin-smooth surface.

With the sandpapering finished and the work thoroughly wiped to get rid of any lingering wood dust, you should be able to consider your carving work finished from the sculpturing standpoint. If you are not entirely satisfied, this is the time to add any finishing touches you feel can and ought to be made.

Then you can stand back and appraise the total result. Let us hope you are liberal enough with yourself to be proud of what you have done but still critical enough to see how you can do better the next time.

sealing the wood's
exposed surface

You now owe the work something that you should get at as soon as possible. In a sense the figure is in a nude state, since the wood's weathered outer covering has been removed. This, odd as it sounds, is not a natural state for it. It is in its most vulnerable condition, a state which was not true of it in nature when it was protected by bark. All its pores are open to attack by its enemies — moisture, change of temperature, insects and fungi.

It needs a protective finish to cover it and seal its pores. Raw wood can absorb moisture all too easily unless it is sealed up promptly. Too much moisture causes cracks and if to moisture is added a rise in temperature the situation becomes dangerous to the wood's health and life expectancy.

THE FRENCH FINISH
AND HOW YOU APPLY IT

A simple way to insure against deterioration is to cover it with what is called a French finish (Fig. 21). The formula is: two parts white shellac and one part alcohol with a few drops of olive oil well mixed in. A "few drops" means ten or fifteen to each ounce of alcohol.

Apply this solution by wetting a soft cloth with it and wiping it on the wood. Make sure every speck of exposed raw wood is covered.

As you apply it you may be concerned because it seems to darken the wood unduly. You will soon see that the finish sinks in and lightens a great deal as it dries. At this stage you receive a bonus in satisfaction. For the first time you are realizing by visual evidence the distinction that can be given your work by the emphasis of the color and grain of the wood. When the last finishing operation is completed the result is even better.

Although the finish seems to dry quickly let it continue to do so for several hours, preferably overnight. Then go over the entire surface you have treated with the finish with some fine steel wool. You remove only the shellac that is on the surface, but not any wood. The place you want the shellac is in the pores of the wood, the minute openings which could otherwise let moisture find its way below the protected surface.

If the subject you have carved is of hard wood it should have two or three coats of French finish which are allowed to dry thoroughly. After each drying rub the surface shellac down with steel wool. If it is of soft wood it will absorb several coats, each rubbed down, before the pores can be considered sufficiently filled to keep out moisture. Never use a piece of steel wool that has become matted and smoothed hard with the shellac it picks up. When a pad or wool gets in that state, so that no clean metal is exposed, discard it for a new pad.

With application of the finish and reasonable care taken to keep the work free from drastic changes in temperature, it is in a condition to last indefinitely, if it is of hardwood, as the old Egyptian pieces have, with the full beauty of the color and the depth and luster of the grain revealed.

The last finishing touch is the use of wax to cover the wood still exposed by the steel wool rubdown, and to attain a gloss or a polish. At one time it seemed to me appropriate to use one of nature's products for this, melted beeswax. It looked well at first but I noticed after awhile that it collected dust and showed finger marks. Now I get better results by wiping on a thin coat of good commercial floor wax with a soft cloth and polishing it with another soft cloth (Fig. 22).

Should you experience the annoyance of a crack or split developing . . . unfortunately this can happen when sculptures are taken from their usual situation and put on view in an exhibition gallery . . . don't be unduly concerned. You can remedy it with the aid of those large chips and some of the dust made by the rasps and sandpaper which you have saved.

HOW TO MEND CRACKS OR SPLITS

If a flaw develops before you have applied the finish, that simplifies things somewhat. Wood opens up when new conditions of rising temperature take place. Often when those conditions are changed back to the kind the wood is happiest in, the crack may close again entirely. If not, mix some of the dust with some Duco cement and force the mixture into the crack with a putty knife or some other kind of knife blade, filling the space as completely as you can.

86

Let it dry well and then scrape off any surplus projecting from the surface of the wood. This will leave the surface the same, or nearly the same, as before the crack appeared. If the filler is applied after the piece has received the French finish and wax, the mended area will, of course, have to receive finish too.

A really wide split or crack can not be mended satisfactorily with the dust and cement mixture. The practical method is to insert a piece of wood in the fissure. Select a large chip that came from the same area in which the split develops and carve and whittle it to fit the crevice as snugly and as deeply as possible. Coat all the inside surface of the split with a good glue and also smear the surfaces of the plug that will be hidden when it is fitted into the fissure. Then pound the plug into place. Do not force it in because that means it is not shaped properly and may just serve to spread the wood a little wider apart. When it fits, let the glue dry a day or two, after which you carve away any protruding surplus. Smooth the surface with whatever abraders are necessary and apply the finish to the raw end of the plug.

I maintain that if a carving is essentially a fine piece of sculpture, no check, crack, split or other mishap can ruin it. A case in point, through a medium other than wood, is the Venus de Milo.

Even fragments of great sculpture retain forever something of the informing spirit of the artist. Wood can be quite as permanent as most materials used by the sculptor and even if one's work is mutilated through some accident of fortune future generations will respond to the truth and beauty of the artist's original concept, as we today respond to the early masters of stone and wood.

tools

A few additional notes on tools, as distinct from how to sharpen them, may be useful.

CHISELS VS. GOUGES

Some kinds of wood carving require the flat chisel. Whenever a carver wants to cut *with* the grain he can remove a good deal of wood rapidly with this type of tool. It acts, in a sense, as a plane blade, but held rigid at a fixed angle and guided by the hand instead of the framework of the plane. The chisel takes off a shaving rather than a chip, making it useful for removing extensive areas of wood or shaving it carefully.

The way I prefer to work, a chisel is not as effective as a gouge in making rounded forms. The chipping action of the gouge, since I always use it against the grain, takes off small amounts of wood at a time and enables a carver to proceed slowly, escaping the misfortune of finding he has taken away too much wood. It also allows him to evolve slowly the form he is working toward and study it more than if wood came away swiftly.

And for cross grain cutting it is easy to comprehend that the gouge, with its scoop shape, cuts a chip that is entirely surrounded on the under side by the arc of the blade so that it comes away cleanly without affecting wood on either side of it. This cannot be done with the flat chisel when large chips are being cut as it would simply tear the wood on either side of the blade.

CUTTER HANDLES

Ash has proved to be the most satisfactory material from which to make chisel handles. Maple is also good. Handle wood must be of good grade and carefully selected by the manufacturer for its function. A carver should make sure that every time he takes up a chisel the blade is firmly attached to the handle and forced into it so that the shoulder of the chisel meets the handle closely.

It is a convenient arrangement to have each chisel handle of slightly different appearance in color and in form (rounded or octagonal). These differences make it easy to recognize the tool you want to reach for in the course of your work.

CARE OF TOOLS

Like any other good tools, those used by a carver last longer and are more satisfactory to work with if they receive a reasonable amount of care.

When putting away tools, such as chisels, give them a light coat of oil, wrap them in a soft, clean cloth and store them in a dry place. If rust should appear it can be removed by rubbing the oxidized area with a soft, clean cloth dampened in a small amount of sweet oil. Put the tool aside and in a few days rub it with finely powdered unslaked lime.

TOOL RACK

A rack is the most convenient way to keep in sight the tools you need most while working. A holder can easily be made by beginning with a board, or boards, of a length that will accommodate the number of tools you want to have handy, and fastening to it a long strip of leather.

First fasten the end of the leather near the end of the board. Then place a tool between the board and the strap to form a loop into which the tool fits comfortably without dropping through and from which it can be easily lifted. Fasten the leather to the board, preserving the loop form, nail it again about an inch farther along to make a space between tools and proceed to form as many loops as are needed. Then fasten the rack to the wall where it will be within convenient reach.

A SET OF BASIC WOOD SCULPTURE TOOLS
AND EQUIPMENT AND MATERIALS

As stated in the text, there is given on page 12 a list of the basic tools for advanced work in wood sculpture. New tools are usually replacements of these or the rare addition of a size or shape not used before. You will find these tools pictured in *Figure 7*.

sharpeners

GRINDERS and whetters for sharpening wood sculpturing tools made of English steel come in three groups ranging from the large and powerful to the small and delicate.

The most powerful type is found in a professional shop, sometimes where tools are sold. It is a large power-driven stone in the form of a thick disk and may be three or four feet in diameter, a large version of the familiar farm, treadle-turned grindstone. The other types are for use in the place where carving is done.

Stones for sharpening tools are so plentiful and well made that there is little excuse for a craftsman to toil away at his work with dull cutting edges. Perhaps those who insist on doing this have the mistaken notion that to keep a really keen edge on a chisel is beyond their powers. The fact is, it is hardly more difficult in the end than not to do it.

Anyone who keeps tool edges keen goes to the professional grinder less often than the person who handicaps himself with half-sharp tools. The exception to this is when a nick appears in a cutting edge which is so deep it must be ground away professionally.

This can happen to anyone, though to a skillful carver probably less often than to one who is only mildly expert.

A wood carver might just as well have cutting edges that are nearly razor sharp. In fact, he had better have them. So many magnified illustrations have been published comparing dull and sharp metal edges that anyone interested in tools knows how nearly even the edge can be made and how surprisingly uneven an edge can actually be and still look sharp to the naked eye. Fine, even edges can be maintained on chisels with the sharpeners required for a sculptor's workshop or studio.

Manufactured sharpening stones and natural ones have their different uses. Those made in an electric furnace have a grit surface harder than stones out of quarries. They take metal off swiftly. Obviously, they are the ones to use first when a cutting edge is pretty well worn. They do the work quickly in the first stage of getting back to a keen edge.

Natural stones are extremely dense and hard. This enables them to produce a very fine edge. The Ozark Mountains in Arkansas supply an abundance of natural stones. Those classed as "soft" rather than "hard" are excellent for wood carving tools.

Wood cutting chisels are ground on the underside to a bevel of 20 degrees to the upper side of the blade and the cutting edge made by a stone that can be held in the hand or laid on a bench is ground at a minutely larger angle.

A gouge and a flat chisel require somewhat different handling in sharpening. A flat chisel is rubbed on a flat, oiled stone with moderate pressure in a leisurely figure eight or oval path.

A gouge cannot be sharpened with this motion. It must be grasped firmly by the blade near the beveled end, the bevel held flat against the stone to be ground from side to side by a kind of rocking motion that drags the bevel against the stone. Apply good pressure and do not rock the hand from side to side. This is accomplished by keeping the forearm in a fixed position and letting it, and the hand, turn or revolve on the axis of the forearm so as to drag the whole surface of the gouge's curved bevel first one way, then the reverse. This may seem like a slow, painstaking process but it takes metal off drastically.

There is a rather new form of gouge sharpener called the India special gouge slip . . . a long, slender cone-shaped form about four inches in length with part of it hollowed out from base to point. This tapering trough varies in width from a couple of inches at the wide end to a quarter of an inch at the point.

The bevelled edge of the gouge is sharpened on it by rocking it from side to side at a place in the trough that accommodates it whether it is a deep or flattish gouge. The outer curved surface of the stone is used to whet the upper flat side of the blade occasionally while grinding the bevel. Care must be taken to keep the blade flat against the stone when doing this to avoid even a minute bevel on the upper side.

A very handy piece of equipment is a small rotary grindstone that can be clamped on a table or bench. The stone is four to six inches in diameter, depending on the make, and is turned by a crank with one hand while the edge to be sharpened is held against it with the other. This takes away metal faster than the block-shaped bench oilstone but more crudely. It is best to ask whether or not a stone of this kind should be kept wet when in use.

It is time to get down to the fine detail of the operation that produces a keen edge by hand.

After a flat chisel, not a gouge, has been ground to the correct bevel, it is necessary to be sure it is square, that is, at a right angle at all points along it to the parallel sides of the blade. This can be accomplished by holding the blade vertically on a flat oilstone and

93

moving it back and forth gently on the part that is out of line. Whether you are attaining a right angle can be tested with a carpenter's square. It is not imperative to have a square edge on a gouge.

Then inspect a flat blade to be sure the flat side of the blade is smooth and even. Rub this, without rocking, on a flat stone with a long oval movement, but for a gouge rock it on a gouge slip.

If it is not certain whether or not the surface of the bevel is flat it must be ground to the correct angle. For a wood carving gouge the surface can be slightly rounded, contrary to the advice of professional sharpeners, as it is a form somewhat stronger than a flat bevel. In making this step toward a keen edge, the bevel is not held absolutely flat against the stone but raised up ever so slightly so that the rotary or rocking motion will grind, or whet, off another bevel, minute in width, at the cutting edge. Not much pressure is required as only a small amount of metal should be removed.

If this last operation is being done properly, so that the extreme edge is being thinned enough to bend, it means that the invisible "wire edge" is forming. It is detected by feeling the edge. This is a sign of good sharpening technique and indicates that the work is nearly done. The wire edge can be felt but hardly seen without a magnifying glass. It is a very fine burr that can be removed by running the edge against a piece of hard wood once or twice. This will break it off.

But it is important that it be broken off cleanly. This is done by continuing to whet the edge until the wire edge wears off and does not leave a root which is a poor foundation for the final razor edge that is expected to last awhile.

To polish up this edge rub it against a fine grain stone, such as one of the small slips, by laying it flat against one of the stone's flat surfaces and raising the chisel very slightly so that the cutting edge is all that rests on the stone. Then stroke rather gently while maintaining the blade at this angle very firmly. Now and then whet the upper side too, a little. A test for the right amount of whetting is to rest the newly-sharpened edge lightly against the thumb nail. If it slides down it is not yet sharp enough. It should be so keen that the edge will catch on the finger nail and not slip.

wood, its structure
and seasoning process

IT is an appealing idea to realize that two of the materials found in nature used by sculptors come from formations that rise to great heights. Just as stone comes from hills and mountains, wood for sculpture comes from the world's highest plants, some of which are nearly as tall as the Washington Monument. A fine piece of wood has the innate appeal that it was a part of a living thing.

Its structure is composed of cells or fibers. Their nature determines whether wood is hard or soft. Hard wood comes from trees that have broad flat leaves, and soft wood from trees with the narrow, resinous foliage familiar to all in evergreens. Some woods have hard exteriors and softer inner cores while in others the opposite is true.

Some woods are heavy and some are light, with a swing from lignum vitae, weighing approximately 89 pounds a cubic foot, to balsa, tipping the scales at between 6 and 8 pounds a cubic foot. But it is interesting to note that any cubic foot of wood when it has all extraneous matter, such as moisture, removed, weighs the same as any other since what is left is simply cellulose. Almost any wood is stronger than iron and some straight grained varieties are eight times stronger than wrought iron, weight for weight. It is also a fact that the weight of wood varies almost from day to day due to fluctuations in its moisture content. That is why dry wood is lighter than moist.

For the purposes of sculpture, it is imperative to work with wood that has been slowly seasoned by the processes of nature; that is, a log stripped of bark and left to season where the temperature varies as little as possible and the wood so stored that air circulates all around it. Keeping it from exposure to rain and direct sunlight, or any other source of direct heat, is a specific situation covered by these requirements.

Under proper conditions the natural moisture which the wood has absorbed in the process of growing will evaporate slowly and gently allow the sapwood to shrink slightly and adjust itself to the changed condition so that it will remain intact if treated well thereafter and be able to resist surprise stresses.

Anyone acquiring wood for sculpture should have heard, at least, of the treatments wood can be given to hasten its drying for commercial purposes; it is a subject that will probably come up in talking with a wood dealer. Speed-up methods are practicable, for instance, in the production of veneers because a cardboard-thin sheet of wood is not subject to the same kind of environmental hazards as is a thick piece of trunk. When a piece of veneer is performing its function it is held securely against another piece of wood, probably laminated, by a strong adhesive. True, it may come unstuck under extreme conditions and thereafter curl or warp, but by then it is too late for cracking or splitting to be important.

Wood can be preserved for years in water, witness piles for piers, and it can be boiled in oil or have oil or wax applied to it. Of course, such treatment diminishes its aesthetic attractions.

There also is an industrial process which impregnates wood

with a material that forms resin, and so changes the wood's physical properties that it is no longer subject to deviations in length, width or thickness when subjected to rapidly changing conditions. A result is to increase the hardness, wearing and polishing qualities without affecting the grain. But one can have grave doubts whether wood so treated would be satisfactory to use for sculpture. At least, I have never had any desire to use it as I feel it has been considerably removed from its natural state.

It can do no harm for sculptors who like working in wood to have some idea of how the forces of nature produce their medium.

The elements of a tree trunk taken in cross section are: the bark, most of which is dead matter but with an inmost layer of living substance; the wood, consisting of sapwood and heartwood; and a small spot at the center of the heartwood, the pith, which is darker than the wood around it.

The basic structure of wood, for our purposes, is the cell. I will not presume to improve on the authoritative way the minute parts of wood's structure are explained in the U. S. Department of Agriculture's *Wood Handbook* which says: "Wood cells are of various sizes and shapes and are more or less firmly grown together. . . . In dry wood the cells are hollow and empty for the most part although some contain deposits of various sorts. Most of the cells in wood are considerably elongated and pointed at the ends, and for that reason are called fibers. The length of wood fibers varies from about one-twenty-fifth inch in hardwoods to from one-eighth to one-third inch in softwoods. The strength of wood, however, does not depend on the length of the fibers, but rather on the thickness and structure of their walls.

"In addition to their fibers, hardwoods have cells of relatively large diameters that comprise the pores, or vessels, through which the sap moves.

98

"In both hardwoods and softwoods strips of cells run at right angles to the fibers, radially in the tree, to conduct sap across the grain. These strips of cells are called rays, wood rays, and medullary rays. In some species of wood the rays are extremely small; in others, such as sycamore and oak, they form the conspicuous flake or silver grain on quarter sawed surfaces.*

"Other cells, known as wood parenchyma cells, store food; they occupy a relatively small volume in most woods. In the softwoods there are no special vessels for conducting sap longitudinally in the tree. The wood fibers, which technically are called tracheids, serve this function. . . .

"Wood is composed of about 60 percent cellulose, 28 percent lignin, and minor quantities of other materials. Cellulose is a colorless material insoluble in ordinary solvents, such as water, alcohol, and benzine, and in dilute acids and alkalies. It forms the framework of the cell wall.

"Lignin is also insoluble in most ordinary solvents but more or less soluble in dilute alkalies. It constitutes the cementing material that binds the cells together and is mixed with cellulose in the cell walls. By dissolving the lignin with suitable reagents the cells may be separated, as in chemical paper-making processes.

"Cellulose and lignin are responsible for many of the general properties of wood, such as its hygroscopicity,** resistance to corrosion by salt water and dilute acids, and susceptibility to decay. These two major constituents are found in about the same proportions in all species, but in addition there are small quantities of other materials in wood, some of which give certain species or groups of species clearly distinctive characteristics. Color, odor, and natural resistance to decay, for example, come from materials other than cellulose or lignin. . . ."

* "Quarter sawed," a veneer term.
** Quality of being sensitive to moisture.

Between the bark and the wood is the substance from which growth emanates. This is cambium. It causes growth in the bark and wood. Year by year new layers of wood are formed on the outer part of the trunk under the bark. Cambium has no influence on wood already formed.

As the cambium performs its function it increases the thickness of the trunk and expands and pushes out the bark. In many kinds of wood new growth can be detected as an annual accretion. This happens in climates where a season, such as winter, retards growth. The character of the cells is altered in a period of seasonal change creating a layer that can often be detected by the naked eye. It is called an annual, or growth, ring. By counting the rings a tree's age can be determined. But in some parts of the tropics, where growth is uninterrupted during the year, the rings are very hard to detect. Under abnormal conditions, such as drought, or unseasonal loss of leaves, a pair of rings are formed, the fainter of which is called a false ring, surrounded by the annual ring.

The fibers which form the body of the wood are too small to be seen without the aid of a high-powered microscope, yet by their size the species to which a piece of wood belongs can be determined. A way to check a classification is by the character of the contents of the pore, which are considered ingrowth and are called tyloses. Their substance gives off a glistening iridescence. The pores of some woods become filled with colored gum which makes another means of identification.

Sapwood contains the living cells which carry on the active part of a tree's life. It is not an immature or unripe substance, as is sometimes inferred from the word, but a mature, living wood until it changes into heartwood as the tree grows. The inactive tissues of heartwood give strength to the trunk.

100

There is no fixed standard stating definitely when a wood is classed as hardwood or softwood. Some woods that are called hard are actually softer than other woods classed as soft. At least it can be said with assurance that conifers — trees that bear cones — are softwoods.

Grain and texture are terms that are used interchangeably. The distinction is that *grain* more often refers to the characteristic appearance of the annual rings, such as fine or coarse grain, and the direction of the fibers that produce a straight, spiral or curly grain; while *texture* refers to the subtler structure of the wood.

Any piece of felled wood will take on or give off moisture from the surrounding atmosphere until the moisture in the wood and in the atmosphere are in balance. If nothing is done to prevent it, wood's moisture content will vary almost daily. The object of seasoning is to cut down the possibility of wide variations, if not to stop them almost entirely. After seasoning, the application of protective coatings can be a very effective way of insuring permanent preservation.

Wood shrinks as it loses moisture and swells as it absorbs it. As a general rule the heavy, hard species shrink more than the soft ones. Proper seasoning does not necessarily mean bone dryness but rather that the material is dried to a proper and uniform moisture content and is free from seasoning defects and internal stresses.

The Department of Agriculture *Wood Handbook* states, on the subject of removal of moisture from wood to season it: "While wood in its green condition as it comes from the tree may contain from 30 to 250 percent water . . . based on the weight of the oven-dry wood, the removal of only the last 25 or 30 percent of this moisture content has the effect of shrinking the wood on drying out; and since wood in service* is never totally dry, the possible shrinkage effect falls within a relatively narrow range. Water is held in the wood in two distinct ways . . . imbibed water in the

* For building purposes.

walls of the wood cells, and free water in the cell cavities. When wood begins to dry the free water leaves first, followed by the imbibed water. The fiber-saturation point is that condition in which all the free water has been removed but all the imbibed water remains; for most woods this point is between 25 and 30 percent moisture content.

"Wood changes size with moisture content only below the fiber-saturation point. Since in seasoning green wood the surface dries more rapidly than the interior and reaches the fiber-saturation point first, shrinkage may start while the average moisture content is considerably above the fiber-saturation point. Wood shrinks most in the direction of the annual growth rings (tangentially), about one-half to two-thirds as much across these rings (radially), and very little, as a rule, along the grain (longitudinally). . . ."

Kiln drying of wood has its advantages for commercial use for furniture. Much wood dried by this method is used, the speedier method having a direct connection with price, an important consideration for large quantity buyers. The drying can be controlled and carried further than the natural method. But when wood is used for sculpture it is better to have it tend to maintain whatever balance it requires with the surrounding air in case any moisture is able to penetrate its protective coating.

The effectiveness of some kinds of coating can be appreciated when it is considered that, taking entirely vulnerable uncoated wood as at zero, three coats of shellac are 87% effective in keeping out moisture and three coats of furniture wax alone are 8% effective. Thus, if furniture wax is applied over three coats of shellac the protective coating over the pores is a good one, although it is not necessarily certain arithmetically that the 87% for shellac plus 8% for wax will add up to exactly 95% effectiveness. It might be more and it might be a little less.

102

The positive statement can be made that wood will not decay if it is kept under the extreme conditions of total absorption . . . that is, submerged in water . . . or, total absence of moisture. It is the condition of *change* in the temperature which can produce an increase of moisture content that brings on decay. Wood deteriorates more readily in warm humid areas than in high altitudes, where lower temperatures allow only a short season in which fungi can develop.

notes on
sculptors' woods

INFORMATION is given in this section on the properties of, and a variety of interesting facts about, woods which are appropriate for sculpture.

WEIGHT

Under the heading "Characteristics" of each wood the weight per cubic foot is supplied. Besides telling the weight of the wood it indicates its relative degree of hardness. The rule is, the heavier the harder.

Wood that weighs under 25 lbs. per cu. ft. can be considered as soft by a sculptor; from 25 to 60 lbs. per cu. ft. as medium to hard; and over 60 lbs. per cu. ft. as very hard.

GRAIN

"Grain" and "Texture" are differentiated as follows: "Grain" denotes the directional arrangement of the fibers and other cells, and is classified as straight, irregular, interwoven, curly, etc. "Roey," which means almost the same thing as "ribbon," refers to the reversible light and dark striping on the radial surface of many woods. Stripes range in width from narrow, as in lignum vitae, to wide, as in mahogany.

TEXTURE

"Texture" refers to the size of the cellular elements and is described as fine, coarse, even, etc.

AVAILABLE COMMERCIALLY

A star (*) after this heading indicates that the wood was at one time imported to this country but is rarely seen now for various reasons, one being the restrictions of governments on its export from its country of origin. They are included, nevertheless, as they may appear again sometime in our markets and because questions about them may come up among sculptors.

Expansions of the terms used after this heading are needed to know just what information they convey:

LARGE LOGS: Over 12 in. in diameter; dealers who cater to sculptors will sell sections or pieces of practicable sizes

SMALL LOGS: Under 12 in. in diameter; usable in long or short lengths

BILLETS: Half logs with bark and heart removed

FLITCHES: See pg. 59; sections cut from logs; if of unwieldy proportions dealers will sell a section from them; some dealers issue price lists of small pieces

LUMBER: Planks up to 4 in. thick; included because the thicker ones are useful for some designs and can also be cut up into smaller pieces

SMALL BLOCKS: Chunks; usually of very rare woods, such as very expensive burls

PROPERTIES OF SCULPTORS' WOODS

ACANA: See Beefwood

AFRICAN BLACKWOOD: See Ebony

AFRICAN GABOON EBONY: See Ebony

AFRICAN MAHOGANY: See Tigerwood

AFRICAN ROSEWOOD: See Bubinga

AFRICAN WALNUT: See Tigerwood

ALMIQUE: See Beefwood

AMARANTH: See Purpleheart

AMARELLO: See Satinwood

AMARILLO: See Boxwood

AMBOYNA BURL: Botanical name, *Pterocarpus nacrocarpus*

Other names: Known to the natives as "kiabocca" wood from the lingoa or kino tree

Related to: PADAUK

Origin: From Amboyna, the largest island in the Molucca Group, popularly known as the Spice Islands in the East Indies

Grain: A complicated network of small rings around the eye of a burl, giving a pebbled appearance

Texture: Hard, firm

Color: One of the world's most startlingly colored woods; rose-reds with backgrounds of light gold; sometimes flashes of scarlet splashed over the surface, occasionally in vivid streaks; the changeable shading varies with changes in the light

Characteristics: Weight 39 lbs. per cu. ft.; dense, medium hard; trees yield logs over 8 ft. in diameter but due to difficulty of transportation from the jungle logs 16 to 28 ft. long and 6 to 8 ft. in diameter are more usual

Uses: In the early 19th Century for furniture and marquetry; now used for panelling and interior trim in luxurious automobile bodies and for novelties; the gum is used for a dye, for the drug kino, and for tanning

Available Commercially*: Small blocks

AMYRIS: See Sandalwood

APPLE: Botanical name, *Pyrus malus*

Other name: GARLAND TREE

Origin: Domestic and foreign

Related to: Pearwood

Grain: Straight to irregular

Texture: Uniform and fine

Color: Reddish brown, medium to low luster

Characteristics: Weight 44 lbs. to 50 lbs. per cu. ft.; tough, strong; easy to work; finishes smoothly; yellowish sapwood; trees sometimes 20 to 30 ft. high and 10 to 12 inches in diameter

History: Has been widely naturalized in North America and is the only member of the genus that supplies commercial timber

Uses: Handsaw and other tool handles, levers, pipes, furniture and turnery

Available Commercially: Small logs

AVODIRE, AFRICAN: See Osage Orange

AXIM MAHOGANY: See Mahogany

BEECH: See Oak, English Brown

BEEFWOOD: Botanical name, *Mimusops spp.* and/or *Manilkara* in the Americas

Other names: BULLETWOOD of British Guiana; MASSARANDA of Brazil; ALMIQUE, ACANA, DONSELLA of Cuba; also known in British Guiana as BULLY, HORSE-FLESH and BALATA TREE

Related to: Silky Oak

Origin: British Guiana and other parts of the northern coast of South America

Grain: Straight; resembles that of beef

Texture: Fine

Color: Red or reddish brown depending on its exposure to air and light

Characteristics: Weight 55 to 75 lbs. per cu. ft.; somewhat brittle, very durable, heavy, strong; not difficult to work; has an oily appearance and feel; finishes smoothly; resists decay in water; among the largest and most massive of tropical trees growing to 100 to 150 ft. with a smooth, straight, cylindrical trunk 5 to 7 ft. in diameter and free of branches for half its height; some species supply a coagulated latex, called balata or gutta percha, which is more valuable than the timber

Uses: Violin bows, arrow footings, furniture, special inlay work, fishing rods; for durable construction such as railroad ties, bridges, posts, poles

107

Available Commercially: Lumber

BLACK MAPLE: See Maple, American Hard

BLACKWOOD (African): Botanical name, *Dalbergia melanoxylon*

Other names: GRENADILLA, MOZAMBIQUE EBONY, SENEGAL EBONY; East India Rosewood is sometimes called Blackwood

Origin: From all parts of India

Grain: Close

Texture: Uniform

Color: Dark purple or plum, almost black

Characteristics: Weight 54 lbs. per cu. ft.; has resonant qualities; free of pores; not hard on tools; receives a polish by their cutting action; free of matter that causes rust

Uses: Clarinets and other musical instruments; surgical instrument handles; a good substitute, commercially, for ivory

Available Commercially: Small logs

BODARK: See Osage Orange

BOIS DE ROSE D'AFRIQUE: See Bubinga

BOMBAY ROSEWOOD: See Rosewood, East Indian

BOWWOOD: See Osage Orange

BOXWOOD: Botanical name, *Buxus sempervirens* (true boxwood)

Other names: AMARILLO, YEMA DE HUEVO (West Indian), INDIAN BOXWOOD, ZAPATERO and JACARANDA (not the hard variety)

Origin: Turkey (true boxwood); other varieties from Venezuela, Brazil, West Indies

Grain: Straight

Texture: Fine and uniform; favorable for carving

Color: Clear yellow; sometimes with a slight greenish tinge

Characteristics: Weight 45 lbs. per cu. ft.; compact; chips very little if the finest tools are used to carve it; resists decay poorly; takes a finish well; from a small tree but not the well-known hedge shrub

108

History: Has been shipped from the Black Sea coast for centuries

Uses: Fine wood engraving blocks, precision rulers, weaving loom shuttles, articles of turnery, flooring; often can be a substitute for maple

Available Commercially: Small logs

BRAZILIAN PINKWOOD: See Tulipwood

BRAZILIAN ROSEWOOD: See also Cocobolo; Rosewood; Satinwood

BRAZILIAN WALNUT: See Imbuya

BROWN EBONY: See Ebony

BROWN OAK: See Oak, English Brown

BUBINGA: Botanical name, *Didelotia africana*

Other names: BOIS DE ROSE D'AFRIQUE, AFRICAN ROSEWOOD, FAUX BOIS DE ROSE DU CONGO

Related to: Rosewood

Origin: West Africa

Grain: Straight and figured, sometimes with a block-mottle

Color: Light violet with dark purple lines

Texture: Fine, even, dense

Characteristics: Weight 55 lbs. per cu. ft.; durable; takes a finish well; comes out of the jungle as large squared-up logs and smaller round ones

Uses: Furniture, pianos, paneling

Available Commercially: Flitches, lumber

BULLETWOOD: See Beefwood

BULLY: See Beefwood

BURMA VERMILLION: See Vermillion

BURMESE ROSEWOOD: See Padauk

CANARYWOOD: See Satinwood

CATALPA: See Primavera

CEDAR: See Thuya Burl

CHERRY: Botanical name, *Prunus serotina*

Related to: Plum and peach

Origin: Domestic and foreign; introduced from Asia Minor (see History below); found in North America from Nova Scotia to the Dakotas and south to the Gulf of Mexico; also down the west coast of South America

Grain: Mostly straight; occasionally has a large roll figure; very large logs may have a blister figure; burls are common thickly studded with eyes the size of pinheads

Texture: Firm, close, uniform

Color: When cut it has a brownish or greenish tinge; on exposure to air and light it changes to a rich reddish brown with a golden luster; narrow, dark, red lines are very evident in a pinkish background in the spring growth; when stained and varnished for the purpose, resembles the color of mahogany

Characteristics: Weight 36 lbs. per cu. ft.; strong; medium density; checks easily; warps very little; long seasoning necessary; old seasoned pieces are good for carving; finishes smoothly; takes a brilliant polish; the most useful is the wild black variety which grows 100 ft. high with a trunk 4 to 5 ft. in diameter; such trees occur infrequently and singly only in moist, rich soil; though once plentiful the supply was drastically reduced by cutting them down to clear land for farms; new logs are now a rarity

History: Cherry trees were introduced into Europe via Rome by a Roman general to commemorate a victory in Asia Minor.

Uses: Originally much used in this country for rail fences and furniture, such as chairs and fine cabinet work; there has been a revived demand for it to make furniture reproductions; also excellent for electrotype blocks

Available Commercially: Large logs

CHESTNUT: See Oak, English Brown

COCOBOLO: Botanical name, *Dalbergia spp.*

Related to: Rosewood, particularly Brazilian Rosewood

Origin: Northern Colombia and parts of the west coast of South America, southern Mexico, Nicaragua, Panama and Costa Rica

Grain: Variable from fairly straight to much interwoven

Texture: Mostly rather fine and uniform, sometimes coarse

Color: Variable; rainbow-hued; lighter colors lose their brilliance after exposure to sunlight and merge into deep red with a black stripe or mottling;

110

colors range through bright red to reddish or purplish brown, more or less distinctly striped; the various shades of red and orange often shot through with bands of jet black; has a medium to high luster

Characteristics: Weight 60 to 75 lbs. per cu. ft.; tough, strong; polishes without wax or oil; resists decay well; feels oilier than most rosewoods; can be turned on a lathe in spite of its hardness; takes on a cold feeling like marble when smoothed; sawdust from it is poisonous like that of satinwood, ivy and sumac; the antidote is a strong solution of 20 Mule Team borax; from a small tree; logs come in crooked, gnarled forms; the most useful supply comes from areas north of Panama and is marketed as solid logs with the sapwood removed

History: Has been important in the cutlery trade for over 50 years

Uses: Knife and tool handles, brush backs; once used for bowling balls; useful in the novelty trade

Available Commercially: Small logs

COFFEEWOOD: See Ebony

CORAIL: See Padauk

CYPRESS: See Thuya Burl

DONSELLA: See Beefwood

EAST INDIAN MAHOGANY: See Mahogany; Padauk

EAST INDIAN SATINWOOD: See Satinwood

EAST INDIA VERMILLION: See Vermillion; Padauk

EBONY: Botanical name, *Disopyros dendo, disopyros sp.*

Other names: MACASSAR EBONY, AFRICAN GABOON EBONY, MOZAMBIQUE EBONY; known also as AFRICAN BLACKWOOD or GRENADILLA, BROWN EBONY, COFFEEWOOD, PARTRIDGEWOOD

Related to: Persimmon

Origin: Africa, Ceylon, Dutch East Indies, South America from or near the tropics, except the persimmon of the U. S. and Japan

Color: "*Black* as ebony" is a popular phrase that does not apply to all ebonies; most of them have a gray or greenish streak; only ebony from the Cape area of South Africa is jet black; it changes in a few months to a brownish black and becomes black when old; some varieties are reddish to greenish

Characteristics: Hard; smooth; takes a polish beautifully; the best commercial ebonies are from India and Ceylon; holly, maple and boxwood are dyed to imitate it; the sapwood changes from white to bluish or reddish after felling

History: Has been an article of commerce for ages

Uses: Ebony and its imitations are used for piano keys and musical instruments, such as violin fingerboards, and for brushbacks, knife handles, rulers, canes, piano cases and other cabinet work, inlays and marquetry

MACASSAR EBONY

Other names: COROMANDEL; named for the city which is the capital of the Celebes in the East Indies; MARBLEWOOD

Origin: Dutch East Indies

Grain: Dense, close

Color: Background of dull black with startling, bizarre markings in mixtures of gray, brown and yellow; sometimes so variegated as to suggest the name Marblewood; stripes are sometimes brown and gray; less suitable than Gaboon Ebony for carving

Characteristics: Weight 69 to 74 lbs. per cu. ft.; logs are liable to be defective; logs shipped 6 to 16 ft. long and pieces 10 to 30 inches long and 16 inches in diameter

GABOON EBONY (African)

Grain and texture: Close

Color: The deepest black obtainable; probably the best of the African ebonies for color

Characteristics: Weight 78 lbs. per cu. ft.; smooth; best variety for carving

Uses: See above under Ebony

MOZAMBIQUE EBONY (African)

Grain and texture: Close

Color: Dark purple

112

Characteristics: Weight 78 lbs. per cu. ft.; cracks easily; liable to contain sandpockets

Uses: See above under Ebony

BROWN EBONY

Other names: PARTRIDGEWOOD, COFFEEWOOD, SOUTH AMERICAN GRENADILLA

Origin: Brazil

Grain: Straight

Texture: Close

Color: Red, dark brown and black: variously mingled in fine hair streaks of two or three shades; the colors supply figure effects

Characteristics: Weight 85 lbs. per cu. ft.; less suitable for carving than Gaboon Ebony

History: Once used in Brazil for ship building

Uses: Cue butts, walking sticks, umbrella handles

Available Commercially: Macassar* — small logs; Gaboon — small logs, billets; Mozambique — small logs; Brown — large logs

ELDER: See Maple

EPPLEWOOD: See Ipil

FAUX BOIS DE ROSE DU CONGO: See Bubinga

FAUX ROSE: See Rosewood, Madagascar

FIG: See Osage Orange

FIRE TREE: See Lacewood

FRENCH ROSEWOOD: See Rosewood, Madagascar

GABOON EBONY: See Ebony

GABOON MAHOGANY: See Mahogany

GARLAND TREE: See Apple

GRAND BASSAM MAHOGANY: See Mahogany

113

GREENHEART: Botanical name, *Nectandra rodioei*

Related to: Myrtle

Origin: British Guiana and other parts of the northern coast of South America

Grain: Straight to roey

Texture: Medium

Color: Light to dark olive or nearly black often with intermingling of lighter, darker areas; silky or silvery luster

Characteristics: Weight 65 to 75 lbs. per cu. ft.; tough, durable, sapwood thick and pale yellow when cut; turning to greenish; hard to cut; easy to split; from a large evergreen tree 70 to 120 ft. high and 2 to 3 ft. in diameter; has a straight, cylindrical trunk buttressed by roots above ground; free of branches 50 to 75 ft.

History: Its value became known in 1796 and the trade in it became one of the principal activities in British Guiana

Uses: Was used in the construction of lock gates and dry docks of the Panama Canal; its resistance to marine worms makes it valuable for piles, wharves, ship siding and other uses where exposure to strain, weather and insects occur; considered the best wood for fishing rods

Available Commercially: Large logs

GRENADILLA: See Blackwood; Ebony

HONDURAS ROSEWOOD: See Rosewood

HORSEFLESH: See Beefwood

IMBUYA (or IMBUIA): Botanical name, *Nectandra*

Other names: BRAZILIAN WALNUT; not a walnut, only similar in color

Origin: Central and South America

Grain: Fairly straight, sometimes curly

Texture: Medium or rather fine

Color: Olive-brown to chocolate-brown; deepens on exposure to air and light; lustrous

114

Characteristics: Weight 43 to 47 lbs. per cu. ft.; strong, durable; easy to work; finishes smoothly; sapwood is yellowish or yellowish-brown; logs come 60 to 80 ft. long

Uses: Fine furniture, cabinet work, interior trim; railroad ties, general construction

Available Commercially*: Large logs

INDIAN BOXWOOD: See Boxwood

INDIA RUBBER TREE: See Osage Orange

IPIL: Botanical name, *Intsia bejuga*

Other name: EPPLEWOOD

Origin: Phillipine Islands; not yet well known

Color: Warm purplish-brown; darkens to almost black with exposure and age

Characteristics: Weight 60 lbs. per cu. ft.; takes an excellent finish; from a large shrub or small tree

History: Just becoming known

Uses: Construction

Available Commercially*: Large logs

IRON MAHOGANY: See Lignum Vitae

IRONWOOD: See Lignum Vitae

JACARANDA: See Boxwood; Rosewood, Brazil

JERICERO: See Primavera

KIABOCCA: See Amboyna Burl

KINGWOOD: Botanical name, *Dalbergia cearensis*, species not named until 1925

Other names: VIOLET KINGWOOD (Acacia Koa); this term is used in the furniture trade as more descriptive but it means Kingwood; the name is applied to several woods that are not Kingwood to lend them prestige

Related to: Rosewood

115

Origin: British Guiana and Brazil

Grain: Finely striped, straight to finely roey; so varied it can create carving problems

Texture: Uniform and fine but the dark layers are a little harder than the others

Color: Violet to deep purple when first cut which fades to a reddish-brown; this accentuates the dark lines which resemble growth rings; alternate layers of violet-brown or blackish-violet; the dark parts are generally narrow and regular; the color patterns may also create carving problems; tones well with age

Characteristics: Weight 75 lbs. per cu. ft.; strong, brittle; can yield a very smooth surface; rings like steel when dropped; the tree is slender and low and 6 inches is a maximum diameter for logs

History: The wood caught the fancy of Louis XIV who ordered it to be used profusely for furniture and other decorative objects which gave it a great vogue

Uses: Furniture veneer, inlay, marquetry and turnery

Available Commercially: Small logs

KINO TREE: See Amboyna Burl

LACEWOOD: Botanical name, *Grevilla robusta*

Other name: SILKY OAK; but it is not oak; one species is called the Fire Tree

Origin: South Queensland and New South Wales

Grain: Some finely figured and silky; others coarse with prominent medullary rays

Texture: Close

Color: Pale pink with a silvery sheen; mottled appearance

Characteristics: Weight 37 lbs. per cu. ft.; strong, tough; easy to work; rays are softer than the rest of the wood which makes finishing a tricky operation; the rays can be stabilized with transparent fillers that will preserve the brightness of the flakes of the silvery sheen of the surface; the thick inner bark forms a sheath-like coarse, woven lace, hence the name; top and bottom stock resembles oak

History: Began to be used outside Australia in the early 1930's

Uses: A few species furnish a good commercial supply but many others have good decorative value; used for small surfaces; popular in Australia for making wagons and carriages as the wood takes nails well; is used as a shade tree on tea plantations in India and Ceylon

Available Commercially*: Large logs

LEMON: See Satinwood

LEOPARDWOOD: See Snakewood

LETTERWOOD: See Snakewood

LIGNUM VITAE: Botanical name, *Guiacum officinale*

Other names: Translated the name means "Wood of Life"; IRON MAHOGANY, IRONWOOD; there is also a common U. S. hardwood called "Ironwood" pieces of which have a maximum diameter of only 5 in.

Origin: Cuba, Haiti, Jamaica, Nicaragua, Guatemala and other parts of the West Indies

Grain: Close and interwoven

Texture: A fabric of fibers tied together to form an interlocked grain of alternating layers which spiral left and right

Color: Varies from olive-brown or olive-green to dark brown or nearly black

Characteristics: Weight 84 lbs. per cu. ft.; one of the three heaviest woods known; cold to the touch when freshly cut and almost immediately begins to exude a green, sticky resin widely used in medicines; it is an enigma to scientists; splits with the greatest difficulty; very durable; oily or waxy; takes a superb finish; excellent for emphasis in broad treatments; one of the best woods for sculpture; from a large, medium-size tree with a short trunk, usually crooked and misshapen; the bark is leathery like sycamore; grows in both arid and fertile soils, the soil apparently causes variation in the thickness of the light yellow sapwood outer cylinder so that it grows from quite thin to as much as a quarter of the diameter of the log; important because logs are not over 3 ft. long with a diameter of 8 in.; a few are 12 ft. long and 20 in. thick; the gum causes the wood to burn with a heat as hot as red-hot iron; it burns like hard coal and leaves the same kind of ash; it cuts readily when green but becomes very dense when thoroughly dry

117

History: In Europe the name was "Life" as the resin was believed to pro-
long life and brought fabulous prices

Uses: Its properties make it very difficult to find even approximate substi-
tutes for it; so hard and durable it is used in ships as a bushing instead of
bronze or steel to carry the propeller shaft through the hull in a jacket
twenty feet long packed with narrow lengths of the wood set end to end
and lubricated with salt water; also used for pulley sheaves and casters;
used some in marquetry but its high oil content makes it difficult for glue
to hold it in place

Available Commercially: Small logs

LINGOA TREE: See Amboyne Burl; Padauk

MACASSAR EBONY: See Ebony

MACASSAR ROSEWOOD: See Rosewood

MAHOGANY: Botanical name, *Swietenia* (true mahogany from the Gulf
of Mexico region); *Khaya ivorensis* (African); classifications of many
woods by the word "mahogany" is controversial; the British Government
lists 75 kinds of mahogany

Other names: GABOON, AXIM, GRAND BASSAM, SECONDEE which are ports of
shipment; other ports would give their name to the wood shipped through
them

Origin: True mahogany is from the West Indies and the best of that is from
Santo Domingo, Cuba and Honduras; also from extreme southern Florida,
Mexico, Colombia and Venezuela; African mahogany grows in many
parts of Africa but the greatest concentration is in a wide belt each side of
the equator in a region along the west coast for several thousand miles

Grain: Finely figured; feather or ribbon; the reason for its great popularity
and wide use

Texture: Fine to rather coarse

Color: Deep, rich red to reddish-brown, pinkish and in some cases yellowish;
high satiny luster

Characteristics: Weight 25 to 50 lbs. per cu. ft. depending on the species;
works easily; takes a beautiful polish and has exceptional cabinet work
qualities; the sapwood is pale yellow or nearly colorless; the African
varieties are considered the best for carving; West Indies trees are smaller
than the African which are huge and grow one tree to six acres; grow

150 ft. high with immense buttress roots, trunks 8 to 10 ft. thick, often clear of limbs for 100 ft.; buttress roots make it necessary to cut trees down from platforms 15 ft. above the ground; trees are spotted by cruising scouts who climb a tree to look over the region with field glasses for the flat green crown resembling that of a walnut tree; felled trees are hewn into square logs in the jungle for reasons of economy and easier transportation to navigable streams on which they are floated to seaports; some logs weigh 10 tons and require the laying of tracks to move them to water all by man power; logs are cut into 30 ft. lengths; the distances between trees has an effect on the variation in weight, texture and color; the wood works well and is free of defects; a log has sold for $12,000 and a trunk of three or four pieces for $20,000

History: The West Indies wood was discovered by Columbus and Drake took a table made of it to Queen Elizabeth; was used by the natives for boats and by explorers for ship repairs; the African woods were discovered 200 years ago and the wood made famous by Chippendale, the great English furniture designer

Uses: Paramount use has been for all kinds of furniture as the handsome and varying grains can be handled in so many different ways, especially as veneers; recommended to wood sculpture beginners to learn the technique of carving although it is considerably softer than the more rewarding hardwoods

Available Commercially: African—large logs, flitches, lumber; West Indies—large logs

MAPLE, AMERICAN HARD: Botanical name, *Acer spp., acer saccarhum* (the sugar maple) and *acer nigrum* (the black maple)

Other names: SUGAR MAPLE, BLACK MAPLE, ROCK MAPLE

Related to: Elder

Origin: Common to U. S. and Canada forests

Grain: Figured; bird's-eye mostly from the Michigan growths

Color: White to reddish brown; in time changes to a warm yellow almost like satinwood

Characteristics: Weight 39 to 49 lbs. per cu. ft.; strong, tough; almost impossible to obtain all white wood as small, dark specks and discoloration are hard to avoid; takes a finish well; the most important wood is from the hard, or rock, maple

119

History: It came into use with the advent of machine tools as it was considered too hard by the early craftsmen to make it into furniture; the outer aspects of curly maple may be deceptive as the surface grain may be plain underneath, and vice versa

Uses: Curly maple became popular for violin backs; provides very hard flooring; frames for implements; vehicles, where strength is important

Available Commercially: Large logs, lumber

MAPLE, OREGON

Grain: Has bird's-eye burl, blister and quilted figure, the latter so-called because of its resemblance to comforter quilting

Color: Light to reddish-brown, sometimes with a faint purplish cast, similar to the eastern U. S. species

Characteristics: Heavy, medium hard; the tree has leaves larger than any other northern tree

Available Commercially: Small logs

MASSANDRA: See Beefwood

MOZAMBIQUE EBONY: See Ebony

MULBERRY: See Osage Orange

MYRTLE: See Greenheart

NARRAWOOD: See Padauk

OAK, ENGLISH BROWN: Botanical name, *Quercus sessiliflora* and *quercus robur* (Pollard Oak)

Other name: POLLARD OAK

Related to: Beech and chestnut

Origin: England

Grain: Straight

Color: Cream white and light tan to dark or leathery brown; a harmless fungus living in the wood works slowly through the grain and medullary

120

rays leaving the wood stained different shades of tan and sometimes a leathery brown with black spots; in very old trees these spots are scattered throughout the wood creating a tortoise-shell effect

Characteristics: Weight 47 lbs. per cu. ft.; durable; checks a good deal in seasoning; takes a finish well; good for general carving; the trunks are immense

History: The name Pollard comes from the word "polled," to cut off or cut short; the oak of England was so coveted by other peoples that they invaded England to get it; to foil them the natives lopped off, or "polled," the tops of whole tracts of them; later the trees sprouted and produced a beautiful special type of wood that came into great favor; England's name was spread over the world in its oak ships; now Pollard oaks are only occasional trees and the wood from them is not necessarily from "polled" trees

Uses: Once had great popularity in this country with the Pullman Company for the decoration of car interiors; has been a staple in English wood carving for a long period

Available Commercially*: Large logs

ORANGE: See Satinwood

OREGON MAPLE: See Maple, American Hard

OSAGE ORANGE: Botanical name, *Toxylon pomiferum*

Other names: BOWWOOD, BODARK from French explorers' Bois d'Arc

Related to: African Avodire, mulberry, fig and India rubber tree

Origin: Red River region of Oklahoma and from Kansas

Color: Yellowish-brown or yellow-orange, golden yellow, sometimes reddish with streaks; has a high luster

Characteristics: Weight 48 lbs. per cu. ft.; the most durable of all the North American timbers; tough, pliable and elastic, strong; takes a fine finish; difficult to work; finishes very smoothly; little affected by changes in humidity; logs 6 to 8 ft. long and 12 to 18 in. in diameter

History: The Indians of the region were the first users

Uses: Wagon wheel rims for dry sandy regions; the Indians considered it the best wood for bows

Available Commercially: Small logs

PADAUK: Botanical name, *Pterocarpus spp.*

Other names: LINGOA, YOMAWOOD, EAST INDIAN MAHOGANY, CORAIL, REDWOOD

Related to: African and Burmese Rosewood, Narrawood, Vermilion

Origin: Andaman Islands in the Bay of Bengal and Burma; a little from West Africa and Central America

Grain: Alternate layers of hard and soft grain, striped, roey and mottled

Color: Sometimes rivals Amboyna; the deep red Andaman sometimes blends in shades of brown and may be the reason it has been called redwood; color changes after exposure to light; some varieties have straw color backgrounds and shades of red streaked with scarlets or red browns

Characteristics: Weight 60 lbs. per cu. ft.; durable; the Burmese wood is the most beautiful and the Andaman the strongest; large open pores characteristic of Rosewood

Uses: Ornamental decorative woodwork, panelling, furniture

Available Commercially: Large logs

PALISANDER: See Rosewood, Brazil

PARTRIDGEWOOD: See Ebony

PEACH: See Cherry

PEARWOOD: Botanical name, *Pyrus communis*

Related to: Apple

Grain: Straight, fine

Texture: Even

Color: Pale yellowish-red

Characteristics: Weight 47 lbs. per cu. ft.; takes a finish well

Uses: Drawing instruments, veneers, marquetry

Available Commercially: Small logs

PERSIMMON: See Ebony

PINE, NORWAY: Botanical name, *Pinus sylvestris*

Origin: Norway
Grain: Even
Texture: Smooth and even
Color: Light cream to reddish
Characteristics: Weight 47 lbs. per cu. ft.; the hardest of the pines; chips easily; softer than tropical hardwoods
Uses: Arrow shafts, furniture
Available Commercially: Lumber

PLUM: See Cherry

POLLARD OAK: See Oak, English Brown

PRIMA VERA: Botanical name, *Tabebuia Donnell-Smithii*. The common name means "Light of Spring" because of the brightness and effect made by the yellow blooms in spring that precede the leaves

Other names: JERICERO or WHITE MAHOGANY; called a mahogany simply because it resembles mahogany in weight and texture but not in color; looks like East India and Ceylon Satinwood
Related to: Catalpa and Brazil White Peroba of the bignonia family
Origin: West coast of Central America, chiefly Guatemala and Mexico
Grain: Varies from plain striped through mottled to highly figured; broken stripe is common
Texture: Medium to coarse
Color: Pale yellow or creamy-white to yellowish-brown with occasional streaks; becomes a rich velvety brown with age like old satinwood
Characteristics: Weight 30 lbs. per cu. ft.; one of the most beautiful of the tropical woods; light, firm; does not warp or check; durable and strong but does not appear to be so; carves well, easy to work; apt to have wood

borer pinholes; the tree grows 50 to 75 ft. high with a smooth trunk 4 ft. in diameter.

History: Shipped to the U. S. before 1892

Uses: Store interior woodwork, furniture and other equipment

Available Commercially: Large logs, flitches, lumber

PURPLEHEART: Botanical name, *Peltogyne paniculata*

Other names: AMARANTH, VIOLETWOOD; called Amaranth for the imaginary purple flower that does not change or fade after cutting

Origin: British Guiana and other parts of the northeast coast of South America

Grain: Straight; sometimes wavy or roey with a suggestion of a mottle figure brought out by finishing

Texture: Fine

Color: Dull brown when cut, which quickly changes to purple; becomes black if exposed to sun and rain; the surface goes through the same phases if a shaving is taken off any time after felling the tree; believed to occur because of oxidation

Characteristics: Weight 62 lbs. per cu. ft.; tough, strong, elastic; an unfinished surface feels harsh; generally excellent for carving; finishes smoothly; takes a high polish; sapwood is white, streaked with purple; the tree grows 125 ft. high and 4 ft. in diameter, clear of branches for 50 ft.; commercial diameters are 2 to 3 ft.

Uses: Furniture, small, fine inlay panels, store fixtures; archery bows and other uses where absorption of heavy shocks is a requirement; in Brazil used for cartwheel spokes; billiard tables, cue butts; is a source of copal, a hard transparent resin necessary in the manufacture of lacquer and varnish bases

Available Commercially: Lumber

QUEBRACHO: Botanical name, *Aspidosperma quebracho-blanco;* the name is a contraction of the native phrase that expresses "axe-breaker"

Origin: Argentina, Paraguay, Brazil

Grain: Irregular, roey

Texture: Fine and uniform

Color: Yellowish or brownish

Characteristics: Weight 70 to 80 lbs. per cu. ft.; one of the hardest known woods; heavy, flinty, strong, brittle, extremely durable; hard to work; takes a high polish; the trees are difficult to transport out of the forest; they grow 30 to 50 ft. high, are 1 to 3 ft. in diameter and are clear of branches for 20 or 30 ft.

Uses: Principally valued for its tannin extract base; balls, turnery

Available Commercially: Small logs

REDWOOD: See Thuya Burl

RIO ROSEWOOD: See Rosewood, Brazil

ROCK MAPLE: See Maple, American Hard

ROSADURA: See Rosewood, Honduras

ROSEWOOD: Botanical name, Brazil R., *Dalbergia nigre;* East Indian R., *Dalbergia latifolie;* Honduras, *Dalbergia Stevensonii;* Madagascar, *Dalbergia Greveana, Baill*

Related to: Padauk; see also Bubinga

BRAZIL ROSEWOOD

Other names: PALISANDER, RIO ROSEWOOD, JACARANDA (not the Brazilian white, hard wood of another family spelled with an acute accent after the last "a")

Origin: Found in Brazil in a belt of land from Rio de Janeiro to Bahia

Grain: Straight, sometimes wavy

Texture: Medium

Color: Chocolate-brown or violet-brown conspicuously streaked with black

Characteristics: Weight 53 to 96 lbs. per cu. ft.; strong durable, sometimes brittle; the most famous of Brazil's woods; has visible pores; finishes smoothly with a high natural polish, if not too oily; the fresh heartwood has a rose-like odor; the sapwood is white or yellowish; liable to have internal flaws; there is considerable waste in the large amount of useless sapwood which reduces logs to 18 to 24 in. in diameter; comes from a 125 ft. high tree of good girth

125

History: Known to commerce for 300 years; once so popular it was called pianowood because of the strong demand for rosewood piano cases and other kinds of furniture made of it

Uses: Spirit levels, plane handles, brush backs, knife handles; it has regained a good deal of popularity in modern furniture and for interior trim and panelling; used for billiard tables, radio cabinets and marquetry

Available Commercially: Large logs, flitches, lumber

EAST INDIA ROSEWOOD

Other names: BOMBAY ROSEWOOD, BLACKWOOD, SISSOO

Origin: All over India

Grain: Very even

Texture: Firm, even, moderately coarse and open

Color: Light canary and straw-yellow tinged with faint red through all shades from red to deep purple

Characteristics: Weight 53 lbs. per cu. ft.; strong; visible pores filled with gum; may have white deposits; gives off a rose odor when cut; logging methods often cause discoloration at the ends of logs; the poorest grades, commercially, are black to dark purple; premiums are paid for the light canary colored wood with pale reddish lines

History: Probably exported before Babylonian times

Uses: Furniture inlays and marquetry; the tree is used to line boulevards in India

Available Commercially: Large logs, lumber

MADAGASCAR ROSEWOOD

Other names: FRENCH ROSEWOOD, FAUX ROSE

Origin: Island of Madagascar off the east coast of Africa

Color: Light to dark rose pink with lines of darker red; a little lighter than Brazilian and East Indian

Characteristics: Very hard; from tall slender trees; logs are less than 9 ft. long

Uses: Furniture decoration; a substitute for tulipwood

Available Commercially: Small logs

HONDURAS ROSEWOOD
Similar to Cocobolo

Other name: ROSADURA

Origin: Central America

Grain and texture: Light, somewhat coarse, dense

Color: Lighter than Brazilian or East Indian; dull brownish to purplish with dark lines or streaks

Characteristics: Weight 58 to 68 lbs. per cu. ft.; strong, tough, durable; has gray sapwood

Uses: Because of its density and resonance it is very useful for the bars of percussion musical instruments such as xylophones and marimbas

Available Commercially: Small logs

For HONDURAS ROSEWOOD see also COCOBOLO and TULIPWOOD

SABICU: Botanical name, *Cojuba arborea*

Origin: Cuba and other parts of the West Indies

Grain: Finely figured, straight and broken roe

Texture: Close and smooth

Color: Chestnut brown; lustrous; sometimes darker, with stripes; the Bahama variety is dark red or reddish-brown; others are purplish

Characteristics: Weight 50 lbs. per cu. ft.; tough, reasonably strong, durable, rather brittle; seasons slowly, shrinks little and does not split; works well; takes a very high polish; sapwood is thin and white; takes exposure to weather well when unpainted or unvarnished; tree 60 to 100 ft. high

Uses: Its fine figure has created a demand for it in cabinet work as it has the properties of mahogany and walnut and can be used as they are; good for flooring, ceilings and ornamental work; used to be used in shipbuilding

Available Commercially: Large logs

127

SANDALWOOD: Botanical name, *Amyris balsamifera*

Other name: Sometimes called AMYRIS

Origin: West Indies and northern South America

Grain: Fairly straight

Texture: Firm, uniform

Color: Yellowish or brownish, more or less streaked; medium to high luster

Characteristics: Weight 62 to 68 lbs. per cu. ft.; strong, durable, brittle, easy to work; has an oily appearance; takes a lustrous polish; sapwood thin and white; produces the fragrant West Indies sandalwood or amyris oil; small to medium size tree

Uses: Principal use is for its oil

Available Commercially: Small logs

SAN DOMINGO SATINWOOD: See Satinwood

SATINWOOD: Botanical name, Brazilian, *Esenbeckia;* East Indian, *Chloroxylon swietenia;* San Domingan, *Zanthoxylon flavum*

Other names: AMARELLO, CANARY WOOD

Related to: Orange and lemon

History: Sheraton called it the king of cabinet woods; he made it as well known as Chippendale did mahogany; it was so hard to work it was not used until 18th Century cutting tools were perfected

Uses: Cabinet work

BRAZIL SATINWOOD

Grain: Straight to decidedly irregular and wavy

Texture: Fine

Color: Beautifully patterned and streaked; yellow or yellowish-brown sometime with pinkish or purplish variegations; fairly lustrous

Characteristics: Weight 56 lbs. per cu. ft.; compact, brittle; easy to work; cocoanut oil odor; takes a high polish; less expensive than the other varieties; tree grows 40 ft. high and 20 in. in diameter; wood has an oily appearance and feel

History: Known to the fine furniture trade for a long time

Uses: Cabinet work, inlays, marquetry

Available Commercially: Large logs

EAST INDIAN SATINWOOD

Related to: The mahogany family

Origin: Ceylon is an important source

Grain: Distinguished by ripple marks

Texture: Dense, smooth

Color: Yellow

Characteristics: Weight 49 to 65 lbs. per cu. ft.; paler and harder than West Indian; Ceylon logs are thick and crooked; grows in torrid jungles

Uses: Turnery, brush backs in Europe and U. S.; bridges, implements and furniture in India

Available Commercially: Large logs, lumber

SAN DOMINGO SATINWOOD

Grain: Irregular, roey, wavy, variously mottled

Texture: Uniform and fine

Color: Molten gold

Characteristics: Weight 51 to 68 lbs. per cu. ft.; fairly durable; easy to work; takes a beautiful polish; gives off a cocoanut oil odor; round logs up to 12 in. in diameter

History: In the 18th Century the best was from Puerto Rico

Uses: Turnery, brush backs

Available Commercially: Small logs

SECONDEE MAHOGANY: See Mahogany

SENEGAL EBONY: See Ebony

SILKY OAK: See Beefwood; Lacewood

SISSOO: See Rosewood, East India

SNAKEWOOD: Botanical name, *Brosium aubletti*

Other names: LETTERWOOD, LEOPARDWOOD

Origin: Dutch East Indies and British Guiana

Grain: Usually very straight; sometimes with a peculiar dark figure resembling a letter or cuneiform writing, as in mahogany; this, and marking suggesting leopard or snakeskin, accounts for the wood's various names; sometimes only vertical stripes with speckles

Texture: Fine, uniform

Color: Rich, dark red or reddish-brown; has a silky golden luster; the letter figure varies from brown to black; color patterns are due to pigment arrangements rather than fibers

Characteristics: Weight 75 to 84 lbs. per cu. ft.; its brittleness causes it to be classed sometimes with the ebonies; hard to cut; splits readily; takes a high polish; finely figured specimens are rare as the logs are small and a large proportion are defective; the sapwood is white or yellowish, thick and very perishable; from a medium size tree 80 ft. high and 30 in. in diameter

Uses: Walking sticks, drum sticks, umbrella and other fancy handles, fishing rod butts, violin bows; inlay work; archery; the Indians used it for their bows

Available Commercially: Small logs

SUGAR MAPLE: See Maple, American Hard

TEAK: Botanical name, *Tectona grandis;* meaning "excellent for construction"

Origin: Burma, Siam, along both coasts of India, the Malay Peninsula, Java and other East Indies islands, and the Philippines

Grain: Even; sometimes finely figured; the wood from Java has the finest figure

Color: Yellow to golden-brown; a golden-brown with variegations when

130

freshly cut; the Javanese variety is the most highly colored with a rich, mellow effect

Characteristics: Weight 45 lbs. per cu. ft.; very durable, takes an exceptional finish; a large majority of the logs are crooked and scarred; some collect a limestone deposit which makes it commercially useless as the deposits dull saws and knives; has an oily surface; feels sticky when first cut; its oiliness causes it to resist decay by water and insects and reduces its expansion and contraction to a low point; it also prevents metal from rusting when in contact with it; it is most accessible in the Burma forests; the tree is tall and slender with enormous leaves and resembles the walnut but for its oil content; the oil gives it a soapy feeling and acts as a preservative; the trees have to be partially dried while standing by girdling them; this causes them to dry enough to be floated to ports of shipment; elephants and water buffalo are very important in the handling of teak in the logging stage

History: Known to world commerce for hundreds of years

Uses: Heavy construction, interior trim, furniture, fine panelling, flooring, carving, architectural woodwork; since metal, such as bolts, against it does not rust, it is valuable for the ribs and decking of ships

Available Commercially: Flitches, lumber

THUYA BURL: Botanical name, *Callistris quadrivalvis*
One of the three true cedars; thuya is the Greek word for sacrifice; given to this wood because oil from it was used in religious ceremonies; the same oil now called sandarac

Related to: Cypress, Redwood

Origin: Morocco, Algeria; on the slopes of the Atlas Mountains

Grain: Very striking; similar to Amboyna; the pinheads that constitute the burl figure are arranged in an infinite variety of patterns some of which can be interpreted as scenery

Color: Rich, deep reddish-brown varying from light to almost black

Characteristics: Weight 19 lbs. per cu. ft.; firm, brittle; has a heavy oil content which provides the fragrant odor; the burning of vast forests by the natives to clear land caused burls to develop on the roots of the burned trees; this is unusual for trees with needle foliage; the burls must be found by grubbing in the ground which is a reason for their scarcity

History: Has been sought after since before the time of King Solomon; Hiram of Tyre helped him to collect enough sweet scented cedar timbers for his famous temple by sending a sea expedition to the Atlas Mountains to cut logs; later, in Greek and Roman times, possession of a piece of furniture made of it, such as a table, was a mark of great wealth; the Moors used it in Spain in the Mosque of Cordova

Uses: Use of this burl in the decoration of a piece of furniture is an indication of the high quality of the piece as the wood is so rare a manufacturer cannot afford to use it for a second grade article; important in the French expensive novelty trade

Available Commercially*: Small blocks

TIGERWOOD: Botanical name, *Lovoa klaineana*

Other names: Once generally called AFRICAN WALNUT because of its color but now called AFRICAN MAHOGANY, to which it is related, when it became the custom in the lumber trade not to use the word walnut for any wood not actually of that family; other names arising from ports of shipment, such as, BENIN and LOVOA

Related to: African Mahogany

Origin: West Africa, Nigeria coast

Grain: Straight, striped and figured

Color: Light golden brown with black streaks varying from dull yellow-brown to the bright gold of satinwood

Characteristics: Weight 34 lbs. per cu. ft.; easily worked; finishes without polish; the pronounced grain and color can create carving problems

Uses: Furniture and interior woodwork; but used more extensively for flooring

Available Commercially: Large logs

TULIPWOOD: Botanical name, *Dalbergia sp.*; formerly classified as *Physocalymma sp.*; the common name was suggested by the similarity of the wood's color to that of a cream and yellow tulip

Other name: BRAZILIAN PINKWOOD

Related to: Rosewood

132

Origin: Brazil, north of Bahia

Grain: Fairly straight to roey

Texture: Rather fine

Color: Striped irregularly with yellow, rose and violet; has a high luster; fades if exposed to strong light but the texture preserves the color after a finish has been applied to the exposed wood; one of the most effectively colored woods varying from yellowish with red or purple stripes and markings to a deep, rose red with a mingling of lighter shades and colors, such as violet and yellow

Characteristics: Weight 56 to 69 lbs. per cu. ft.; one of the rarest and best known Brazilian woods; strong; mildly fragrant scent; not easy to work; splinters; takes a high natural polish; a small tree; the trunks are irregular and slender; liable to have defective heartwood

History: Known to European cabinetmakers for years and a favorite in France in the Empire period

Uses: Turnery, cabinetmaking; marquetry, brush backs

Available Commercially: Small logs

VERMILLION: Botanical name, *Pterocarpus macro carpus*

See PADAUK

Other names: EAST INDIA or BURMA VERMILLION

Color: Dark vermillion to a light pinkish cast

Available Commercially: Large logs

VIOLET KINGWOOD: See Kingwood

VIOLETWOOD: See Purpleheart

WALNUT: Botanical name, *Juglans family;* a large group embracing Black American W., California W., Circassian W., East Indian W. or Laurel, English W., French W., Italian W., Queensland W., satin (gum), white, or butternut

Related to: Hickory and butternut

Origin: Widespread in temperate climates as indicated above after the name

Grain: Mostly straight

133

Texture: Medium

Color: Deep reddish-brown or chocolate; somewhat variegated; somewhat lustrous

Characteristics: Weight 28 to 49 lbs. per cu. ft.; fairly strong, durable; the effect of a cutting tool leaves a finish that is little improved by polishing; fresh wood has distinctive odor; easy to work; has gray sapwood

History: One of the oldest woods used for ornamental purposes; became popular in pre-Renaissance Italy

Uses: Wood carving; gun and rifle stocks; airplane propellers

Available Commercially: American — Large logs, small logs, flitches; lumber

WHITE MAHOGANY: See Primavera

WHITE PEROBA: See Primavera

WHITEWOOD: See Palo Blanco

YEMA DE HUEVO: See Boxwood

YOMAWOOD: See Padauk

ZAPATERO: See Boxwood

134

table of relative hardness
and color of woods

THE table below will serve as a quick reference to help the sculptor determine which type of wood is appropriate for the subject he intends to carve. Since relative hardness and color are the primary considerations, only these two characteristics are given. The woods are arranged in order from the softest to the hardest.

NAME OF WOOD VARIETY	WEIGHT PER CU. FT. IN LBS.	COLOR
Thuya Burl	19	Brown (deep reddish) varying from light to almost black
Walnut	28–49	Brown (deep reddish or chocolate)
Mahogany	25–50	Red (deep, rich) to reddish-brown, pinkish or yellowish
Primavera	30	Yellow (pale) or creamy white to yellowish-brown with streaks; in time, a rich velvety brown
Tigerwood	34	Brown (light golden) from dull yellow-brown to bright gold, with black streaks
Cherry	36	Brown (rich reddish)
Lacewood	37	Pink (pale) with a silvery sheen
Amboyna Burl	39	Reds, variegated and startling with gold background
Maple, American Hard	39–49	White to reddish-brown; in time changes to a warm yellow

NAME OF WOOD VARIETY	WEIGHT PER CU. FT. IN LBS.	COLOR
Maple, Oregon		Brown (light to reddish), purple-cast
Imbuya	43–47	Brown (olive to chocolate)
Apple	44–50	Brown (reddish)
Boxwood	45	Yellow
Teak	45	Yellow to golden brown
Oak, English Brown	47	Cream white and light tan to dark or leathery brown
Pearwood	47	Red (pale yellowish)
Pine, Norway	47	Cream (light) to reddish
Osage Orange	48	Yellowish-brown, yellow-orange, golden yellow, red; with streaks
Satinwood, East Indian	49–65	Yellow
Sabicu	50	Brown (chestnut) and reddish-brown, or dark red, or purplish
Satinwood, San Domingo	51–68	Gold
Rosewood, East Indian	53	Yellow (canary to straw) with faint tinges of red to deep purple
Rosewood, Brazil	54	Brown (chocolate or violet) streaked with black
Blackwood	54	Purple or plum, dark, almost black
Bubinga	55	Violet (light) and dark purple
Beefwood	55–75	Reddish or brownish
Satinwood, Brazil	56	Yellow, yellowish-brown, sometimes with pinkish or purplish variegation
Tulipwood	56–69	Yellow, rose and violet; irregular striping
Rosewood, Honduras	58–68	Brown (dull) to purplish with dark streaks
Padauk	60	Red, brown or straw in startling combinations